MznLnx

Missing Links Exam Preps

Exam Prep for

Operations Management

Stevenson, 9th Edition

The MznLnx Exam Prep is your link from the texbook and lecture to your exams.
The MznLnx Exam Preps are unauthorized and comprehensive reviews of your textbooks.

All material provided by MznLnx and Rico Publications (c) 2010
Textbook publishers and textbook authors do not particpate in or contribute to these reviews.

MznLnx

Rico Publications

Exam Prep for Operations Management
9th Edition
Stevenson

Publisher: Raymond Houge	*Product Manager:* Dave Mason
Assistant Editor: Michael Rouger	*Editorial Assitant:* Rachel Guzmanji
Text and Cover Designer: Lisa Buckner	*Pedagogy:* Debra Long
Marketing Manager: Sara Swagger	*Cover Image:* Jim Reed/Getty Images
Project Manager, Editorial Production: Jerry Emerson	*Text and Cover Printer:* City Printing, Inc.
Art Director: Vernon Lowerui	*Compositor:* Media Mix, Inc.

(c) 2010 Rico Publications

ALL RIGHTS RESERVED. No part of this work covered by the copyright may be reproduced or used in any form or by an means--graphic, electronic, or mechanical, including photocopying, recording, taping, Web distribution, information storage, and retrieval systems, or in any other manner--without the written permission of the publisher.

Printed in the United States
ISBN:

For more information about our products, contact us at:
Dave.Mason@RicoPublications.com

For permission to use material from this text or product, submit a request online to:
Dave.Mason@RicoPublications.com

Contents

CHAPTER 1
Introduction to Operations Management — 1

CHAPTER 2
Competitiveness, Strategy, and Productivity — 16

CHAPTER 3
Forecasting — 23

CHAPTER 4
Product and Service Design — 31

CHAPTER 5
Strategic Capacity Planning for Products and Services — 37

CHAPTER 6
Process Selection and Facility Layout — 48

CHAPTER 7
Design of Work Systems — 57

CHAPTER 8
Location Planning and Analysis — 61

CHAPTER 9
Management of Quality — 65

CHAPTER 10
Quality Control — 73

CHAPTER 11
Supply Chain Management — 78

CHAPTER 12
Inventory Management — 87

CHAPTER 13
Aggregate Planning — 93

CHAPTER 14
MRP and ERP — 98

CHAPTER 15
JIT and Lean Operations — 102

CHAPTER 16
Scheduling — 109

CHAPTER 17
Project Management — 112

CHAPTER 18
Management of Waiting Lines — 117

ANSWER KEY — 119

TO THE STUDENT

COMPREHENSIVE

The *MznLnx* Exam Prep series is designed to help you pass your exams. Editors at MznLnx review your textbooks and then prepare these practice exams to help you master the textbook material. Unlike study guides, workbooks, and practice tests provided by the texbook publisher and textbook authors, *MznLnx* gives you **all** of the material in each chapter in exam form, not just samples, so you can be sure to nail your exam.

MECHANICAL

The MznLnx Exam Prep series creates exams that will help you learn the subject matter as well as test you on your understanding. Each question is designed to help you master the concept. Just working through the exams, you gain an understanding of the subject--its a simple mechanical process that produces success.

INTEGRATED STUDY GUIDE AND REVIEW

MznLnx is not just a set of exams designed to test you, its also a comprehensive review of the subject content. Each exam question is also a review of the concept, making sure that you will get the answer correct without having to go to other sources of material. You learn as you go! Its the easiest way to pass an exam.

HUMOR

Studying can be tedious and dry. MznLnx's instructional design includes moderate humor within the exam questions on occassion, to break the tedium and revitalize the brain

Chapter 1. Introduction to Operations Management

1. _____ is one of the managerial functions like planning, organizing, staffing and directing. It is an important function because it helps to check the errors and to take the corrective action so that deviation from standards are minimized and stated goals of the organization are achieved in desired manner. According to modern concepts, _____ is a foreseeing action whereas earlier concept of _____ was used only when errors were detected. _____ in management means setting standards, measuring actual performance and taking corrective action.

   a. Turnover
   b. Control
   c. Schedule of reinforcement
   d. Decision tree pruning

2. A _____ is a change implemented to address a weakness identified in a management system. Normally _____s are implemented in response to a customer complaint, abnormal levels of internal nonconformity, nonconformities identified during an internal audit or adverse or unstable trends in product and process monitoring such as would be identified by SPC.

   The process of determining a _____ requires identification of actions that can be taken to prevent or mitigate the weakness.

   a. 1990 Clean Air Act
   b. 28-hour day
   c. Zero defects
   d. Corrective action

3. _____ describes the situation when output from (or information about the result of) an event or phenomenon in the past will influence the same event/phenomenon in the present or future. When an event is part of a chain of cause-and-effect that forms a circuit or loop, then the event is said to 'feed back' into itself.

   _____ is also a synonym for:

   - _____ signal; the information about the initial event that is the basis for subsequent modification of the event.
   - _____ loop; the causal path that leads from the initial generation of the _____ signal to the subsequent modification of the event.

   _____ is a mechanism, process or signal that is looped back to control a system within itself. Such a loop is called a _____ loop.

   a. Positive feedback
   b. Feedback loop
   c. 1990 Clean Air Act
   d. Feedback

4. _____ is an integrated communications-based process through which individuals and communities discover that existing and newly-identified needs and wants may be satisfied by the products and services of others.

   _____ is defined by the American _____ Association as the activity, set of institutions, and processes for creating, communicating, delivering, and exchanging offerings that have value for customers, clients, partners, and society at large. The term developed from the original meaning which referred literally to going to market, as in shopping, or going to a market to buy or sell goods or services.

Chapter 1. Introduction to Operations Management

    a. Marketing
    b. Customer relationship management
    c. Market development
    d. Disruptive technology

5. _____ is an area of business concerned with the production of goods and services, and involves the responsibility of ensuring that business operations are efficient in terms of using as little resource as needed, and effective in terms of meeting customer requirements. It is concerned with managing the process that converts inputs (in the forms of materials, labour and energy) into outputs (in the form of goods and services.)

Operations traditionally refers to the production of goods and services separately, although the distinction between these two main types of operations is increasingly difficult to make as manufacturers tend to merge product and service offerings.

    a. AAAI
    b. A4e
    c. A Stake in the Outcome
    d. Operations management

6. _____ is a form of communication that typically attempts to persuade potential customers to purchase or to consume more of a particular brand of product or service. 'While now central to the contemporary global economy and the reproduction of global production networks, it is only quite recently that _____ has been more than a marginal influence on patterns of sales and production. The formation of modern _____ was intimately bound up with the emergence of new forms of monopoly capitalism around the end of the 19th and beginning of the 20th century as one element in corporate strategies to create, organize and where possible control markets, especially for mass produced consumer goods.
    a. Advertising
    b. A Stake in the Outcome
    c. AAAI
    d. A4e

7. _____ is a term defined by the Oxford English Dictionary as an individual's 'course or progress through life '. It is usually considered to pertain to remunerative work (and sometimes also formal education.)

The etymology of the term is somewhat ironic in that it comes from the Latin word carrera, which means race .

    a. Career planning
    b. Spatial mismatch
    c. Nursing shortage
    d. Career

8. A _____ is a list of the general tasks and responsibilities of a position. Typically, it also includes to whom the position reports, specifications such as the qualifications needed by the person in the job, salary range for the position, etc. A _____ is usually developed by conducting a job analysis, which includes examining the tasks and sequences of tasks necessary to perform the job.
    a. Recruitment
    b. Job description
    c. Recruitment advertising
    d. Recruitment Process Insourcing

9. _____ refers to the difference between the cost of materials purchased by a company plus the cost of the labor to assemble a product and the price at which the company sells the product. An example is the price of gasoline at the pump over the price of the oil in it. In national accounts used in macroeconomics, it refers to the contribution of the factors of production, i.e., land, labor, and capital goods, to raising the value of a product and corresponds to the incomes received by the owners of these factors.

Chapter 1. Introduction to Operations Management

a. Rehn-Meidner Model
c. Value added
b. Deregulation
d. Minimum wage

10. _____ is an advertisement in which a particular product specifically mentions a competitor by name for the express purpose of showing why the competitor is inferior to the product naming it.

This should not be confused with parody advertisements, where a fictional product is being advertised for the purpose of poking fun at the particular advertisement, nor should it be confused with the use of a coined brand name for the purpose of comparing the product without actually naming an actual competitor. ('Wikipedia tastes better and is less filling than the Encyclopedia Galactica.')

In the 1980s, during what has been referred to as the cola wars, soft-drink manufacturer Pepsi ran a series of advertisements where people, caught on hidden camera, in a blind taste test, chose Pepsi over rival Coca-Cola.

a. Comparative advertising
c. 1990 Clean Air Act
b. 33 Strategies of War
d. 28-hour day

11. _____ refers to metrics and measures of output from production processes, per unit of input. Labor _____, for example, is typically measured as a ratio of output per labor-hour, an input. _____ may be conceived of as a metrics of the technical or engineering efficiency of production.

a. Master production schedule
c. Productivity
b. Value engineering
d. Remanufacturing

12. _____ is a contract between two parties, one being the employer and the other being the employee. An employee may be defined as: 'A person in the service of another under any contract of hire, express or implied, oral or written, where the employer has the power or right to control and direct the employee in the material details of how the work is to be performed.' Black's Law Dictionary page 471 (5th ed. 1979.)

a. Employment
c. Exit interview
b. Employment counsellor
d. Employment rate

13. _____ is a family of standards for quality management systems. _____ is maintained by ISO, the International Organization for Standardization and is administered by accreditation and certification bodies. The rules are updated, the time and changes in the requirements for quality, motivate change.

a. A4e
c. A Stake in the Outcome
b. AAAI
d. ISO 9000

14. _____ is an operational activity which does an aggregate plan for the production process, in advance of 2 to 18 months, to give an idea to management as to what quantity of materials and other resources are to be procured and when, so that the total cost of operations of the organization is kept to the minimum over that period.

The quantity of outsourcing, subcontracting of items, overtime of labor, numbers to be hired and fired in each period and the amount of inventory to be held in stock and to be backlogged for each period are decided. All of these activities are done within the framework of the company ethics, policies, and long term commitment to the society, community and the country of operation.

Chapter 1. Introduction to Operations Management

   a. Earned Schedule
   c. A Stake in the Outcome
   b. Aggregate planning
   d. Earned value management

15. _____ is the process of estimation in unknown situations. Prediction is a similar, but more general term. Both can refer to estimation of time series, cross-sectional or longitudinal data.
   a. 1990 Clean Air Act
   c. 33 Strategies of War
   b. 28-hour day
   d. Forecasting

16. A _____ is a set of sequential operations established in a factory whereby materials are put through a refining process to produce an end-product that is suitable for onward consumption; or components are assembled to make a finished article.

Typically, raw materials such as metal ores or agricultural products such as foodstuffs or textile source plants (cotton, flax) require a sequence of treatments to render them useful. For metal, the processes include crushing, smelting and further refining.

   a. Production line
   c. Six Sigma
   b. Theory of constraints
   d. Takt time

17. In engineering and manufacturing, _____ and quality engineering are used in developing systems to ensure products or services are designed and produced to meet or exceed customer requirements. Refer to the definition by Merriam-Webster for further information . These systems are often developed in conjunction with other business and engineering disciplines using a cross-functional approach.
   a. Statistical process control
   c. Process capability
   b. Quality control
   d. Single Minute Exchange of Die

18. An _____ is a manufacturing process in which parts (usually interchangeable parts) are added to a product in a sequential manner using optimally planned logistics to create a finished product much faster than with handcrafting-type methods. The _____ developed by Ford Motor Company between 1908 and 1915 made _____s famous in the following decade through the social ramifications of mass production, such as the affordability of the Ford Model T and the introduction of high wages for Ford workers. However, the various preconditions for the development at Ford stretched far back into the 19th century, from the gradual realization of the dream of interchangeability, to the concept of reinventing workflow and job descriptions using analytical methods.
   a. A4e
   c. A Stake in the Outcome
   b. AAAI
   d. Assembly line

19. _____ is one of the four elements of marketing mix. An organization or set of organizations (go-betweens) involved in the process of making a product or service available for use or consumption by a consumer or business user.

The other three parts of the marketing mix are product, pricing, and promotion.

   a. Missing completely at random
   c. Distribution
   b. Matching theory
   d. Job creation programs

20. _____ is also known as operations management, management science, systems engineering, or manufacturing engineering; a distinction that seems to depend on the viewpoint or motives of the user. Recruiters or educational establishments use the names to differentiate themselves from others. In healthcare, for example, industrial engineers are more commonly known as management engineers or health systems engineers.

   a. A Stake in the Outcome   b. A4e
   c. AAAI   d. Industrial engineering

21. _____ can be regarded as an outcome of mental processes (cognitive process) leading to the selection of a course of action among several alternatives. Every _____ process produces a final choice. The output can be an action or an opinion of choice.

   a. 28-hour day   b. 33 Strategies of War
   c. 1990 Clean Air Act   d. Decision making

22. _____ is the process of determining the production capacity needed by an organization to meet changing demands for its products. In the context of _____, 'capacity' is the maximum amount of work that an organization is capable of completing in a given period of time.

A discrepancy between the capacity of an organization and the demands of its customers results in inefficiency, either in under-utilized resources or unfulfilled customers.

   a. Remanufacturing   b. Scientific management
   c. Productivity   d. Capacity planning

23. _____ of the learning curve effect and the closely related experience curve effect express the relationship between equations for experience and efficiency or between efficiency gains and investment in the effort. The experience of 'learning curves' was first observed by the 19th Century German psychologist Hermann Ebbinghaus according to the difficulty of memorizing varying numbers of verbal stimuli, and subsequent learning about the complex processes of learning are discussed in the

.

The rule used for representing the learning curve effect states that the more times a task has been performed, the less time will be required on each subsequent iteration.

   a. Spatial Decision Support Systems   b. Distribution
   c. Models   d. Point biserial correlation coefficient

24. A _____ is a set of mathematical equations which describe the behavior of an object of study in terms of random variables and their associated probability distributions. If the model has only one equation it is called a single-equation model, whereas if it has more than one equation, it is known as a multiple-equation model.

In mathematical terms, a _____ is frequently thought of as a pair (Y,P) where Y is the set of possible observations and P the set of possible probability distributions on Y.

Chapter 1. Introduction to Operations Management

a. 28-hour day
b. 1990 Clean Air Act
c. Statistical model
d. 33 Strategies of War

25. The _____, is a mathematically based algorithm for scheduling a set of project activities. It is an important tool for effective project management.

It was developed in the 1950s by the Dupont Corporation at about the same time that General Dynamics and the US Navy were developing the Program Evaluation and Review Technique (PERT) Today, it is commonly used with all forms of projects, including construction, software development, research projects, product development, engineering, and plant maintenance, among others.

a. 33 Strategies of War
b. 28-hour day
c. 1990 Clean Air Act
d. Critical path method

26. A _____ is a type of bar chart that illustrates a project schedule. _____ s illustrate the start and finish dates of the terminal elements and summary elements of a project. Terminal elements and summary elements comprise the work breakdown structure of the project.

a. 1990 Clean Air Act
b. 33 Strategies of War
c. Gantt chart
d. 28-hour day

27. In mathematics, _____ is a technique for optimization of a linear objective function, subject to linear equality and linear inequality constraints. Informally, _____ determines the way to achieve the best outcome (such as maximum profit or lowest cost) in a given mathematical model and given some list of requirements represented as linear equations.

More formally, given a polytope (for example, a polygon or a polyhedron), and a real-valued affine function

$$f(x_1, x_2, \ldots, x_n) = c_1 x_1 + c_2 x_2 + \cdots + c_n x_n + d$$

defined on this polytope, a _____ method will find a point in the polytope where this function has the smallest (or largest) value.

a. 1990 Clean Air Act
b. Linear programming
c. Slack variable
d. Linear programming relaxation

28. The Program (or Project) Evaluation and Review Technique, commonly abbreviated _____, is a model for project management designed to analyze and represent the tasks involved in completing a given project.

_____ is a method to analyze the involved tasks in completing a given project, specially the time needed to complete each task, and identifying the minimum time needed to complete the total project.

_____ was developed primarily to simplify the planning and scheduling of large and complex projects.

a. 28-hour day
b. 33 Strategies of War
c. 1990 Clean Air Act
d. PERT

Chapter 1. Introduction to Operations Management

29. _____ refers to the movement of cash into or out of a business or financial product. It is usually measured during a specified, finite period of time. Measurement of _____ can be used

- to determine a project's rate of return or value. The time of _____s into and out of projects are used as inputs in financial models such as internal rate of return, and net present value.
- to determine problems with a business's liquidity. Being profitable does not necessarily mean being liquid. A company can fail because of a shortage of cash, even while profitable.
- as an alternate measure of a business's profits when it is believed that accrual accounting concepts do not represent economic realities. For example, a company may be notionally profitable but generating little operational cash (as may be the case for a company that barters its products rather than selling for cash.) In such a case, the company may be deriving additional operating cash by issuing shares evaluating default risk, re-investment requirements, etc.

_____ is a generic term used differently depending on the context. It may be defined by users for their own purposes.

a. Cash flow	b. Gross profit
c. Sweat equity	d. Gross profit margin

30. In economics, business, retail, and accounting, a _____ is the value of money that has been used up to produce something, and hence is not available for use anymore. In economics, a _____ is an alternative that is given up as a result of a decision. In business, the _____ may be one of acquisition, in which case the amount of money expended to acquire it is counted as _____.

a. Cost overrun	b. Fixed costs
c. Cost allocation	d. Cost

31. _____ is an increasingly broadening term with which an organization, or other human system describes the combination of traditionally administrative personnel functions with acquisition and application of skills, knowledge and experience, Employee Relations and resource planning at various levels. The field draws upon concepts developed in Industrial/Organizational Psychology and System Theory. _____ has at least two related interpretations depending on context. The original usage derives from political economy and economics, where it was traditionally called labor, one of four factors of production although this perspective is changing as a function of new and ongoing research into more strategic approaches at national levels. This first usage is used more in terms of '_____ development', and can go beyond just organizations to the level of nations . The more traditional usage within corporations and businesses refers to the individuals within a firm or agency, and to the portion of the organization that deals with hiring, firing, training, and other personnel issues, typically referred to as `_____ management'.

a. Human resources	b. Bradford Factor
c. Progressive discipline	d. Human resource management

32. Industrial engineering is also known as operations management, management science, systems engineering, or manufacturing engineering; a distinction that seems to depend on the viewpoint or motives of the user. Recruiters or educational establishments use the names to differentiate themselves from others. In healthcare, for example, _____ are more commonly known as management engineers or health systems engineers.

a. A4e	b. AAAI
c. A Stake in the Outcome	d. Industrial Engineers

Chapter 1. Introduction to Operations Management

33. _____, is the discipline of using scientific research-based principles, strategies, and other analytical methods, such as mathematical modeling to improve any organization's ability to enact rational, meaningful business management decisions.
    a. Cross ownership
    b. Workflow
    c. Trustee
    d. Management Science

34. _____ in the USA, Canada, South Africa and Australia, and operational research in Europe, is an interdisciplinary branch of applied mathematics and formal science that uses methods such as mathematical modeling, statistics, and algorithms to arrive at optimal or near optimal solutions to complex problems. It is typically concerned with optimizing the maxima (profit, assembly line performance, crop yield, bandwidth, etc) or minima (loss, risk, etc.) of some objective function.
    a. A Stake in the Outcome
    b. A4e
    c. AAAI
    d. Operations Research

35. _____ is the discipline of planning, organizing and managing resources to bring about the successful completion of specific project goals and objectives. It is often closely related to and sometimes conflated with Program management.

A project is a finite endeavor--having specific start and completion dates--undertaken to meet particular goals and objectives, usually to bring about beneficial change or added value.

    a. Work package
    b. Project Management
    c. Precedence diagram
    d. Project engineer

36. The _____ is a non-profit professional organization with the purpose of advancing the state-of-the-art of project management. The company is a professional association for the project management profession.

The _____ Inc.

    a. 1990 Clean Air Act
    b. 28-hour day
    c. 33 Strategies of War
    d. Project Management Institute

37. _____ is the practice of managing the flow of information between an organization and its publics. _____ gains an organization or individual exposure to their audiences using topics of public interest and news items that do not require direct payment. Because _____ places exposure in credible third-party outlets, it offers a third-party legitimacy that advertising does not have.
    a. 28-hour day
    b. Public relations
    c. Two-way communication
    d. 1990 Clean Air Act

38. _____, in microeconomics, are the cost advantages that a business obtains due to expansion. They are factors that cause a producer's average cost per unit to fall as scale is increased. _____ is a long run concept and refers to reductions in unit cost as the size of a facility, or scale, increases.
    a. A Stake in the Outcome
    b. A4e
    c. Economies of scale
    d. Economies of scope

Chapter 1. Introduction to Operations Management

39. The _____ was a period in the late 18th and early 19th centuries when major changes in agriculture, manufacturing, mining, and transportation had a profound effect on the socioeconomic and cultural conditions in Britain. The changes subsequently spread throughout Europe, North America, and eventually the world. The onset of the _____ marked a major turning point in human society; almost every aspect of daily life was eventually influenced in some way.
   a. Affiliation
   b. Adam Smith
   c. Abraham Harold Maslow
   d. Industrial Revolution

40. A _____ is a computer program typically used to provide some form of artificial intelligence, which consists primarily of a set of rules about behavior. These rules, termed productions, are a basic representation found useful in AI planning, expert systems and action selection. A _____ provides the mechanism necessary to execute productions in order to achieve some goal for the system.
   a. 1990 Clean Air Act
   b. 33 Strategies of War
   c. Production system
   d. 28-hour day

41. _____ is a theory of management that analyzes and synthesizes workflows, with the objective of improving labour productivity. The core ideas of the theory were developed by Frederick Winslow Taylor in the 1880s and 1890s, and were first published in his monographs, Shop Management and The Principles of _____ Taylor believed that decisions based upon tradition and rules of thumb should be replaced by precise procedures developed after careful study of an individual at work.
   a. Capacity planning
   b. Master production schedule
   c. Value engineering
   d. Scientific management

42. _____, widely known as F. W. Taylor, was an American mechanical engineer who sought to improve industrial efficiency. He is regarded as the father of scientific management, and was one of the first management consultants.

Taylor was one of the intellectual leaders of the Efficiency Movement and his ideas, broadly conceived, were highly influential in the Progressive Era.

   a. Frederick Winslow Taylor
   b. Jonah Jacob Goldberg
   c. Geoffrey Colvin
   d. Douglas N. Daft

43. _____ are parts that are for practical purposes identical. They are made to specifications that ensure that they are so nearly identical that they will fit into any device of the same type. One such part can freely replace another, without any custom fitting (such as filing.)
   a. A4e
   b. A Stake in the Outcome
   c. AAAI
   d. Interchangeable parts

44. _____ is an inventory strategy that strives to improve the return on investment of a business by reducing in-process inventory and its associated carrying costs. To meet _____ objectives, the process relies on signals between different points in the process. This means the process is often driven by a series of signals, or Kanban , which tell production when to make the next part. Kanban are usually 'tickets' but can be simple visual signals, such as the presence or absence of a part on a shelf. Implemented correctly, _____ can dramatically improve a manufacturing organization's return on investment, quality, and efficiency.
   a. 1990 Clean Air Act
   b. 33 Strategies of War
   c. 28-hour day
   d. Just-in-time

45. _____ or lean production, which is often known simply as 'Lean', is a production practice that considers the expenditure of resources for any goal other than the creation of value for the end customer to be wasteful, and thus a target for elimination. Working from the perspective of the customer who consumes a product or service, 'value' is defined as any action or process that a customer would be willing to pay for. Basically, lean is centered around creating more value with less work.
   a. Production line
   b. Six Sigma
   c. Theory of constraints
   d. Lean manufacturing

46. _____ is the production of large amounts of standardized products, including and especially on assembly lines. The concepts of _____ are applied to various kinds of products, from fluids and particulates handled in bulk to discrete solid parts to assemblies of such parts

_____ of assemblies typically uses electric-motor-powered moving tracks or conveyor belts to move partially complete products to workers, who perform simple repetitive tasks.

   a. 33 Strategies of War
   b. 1990 Clean Air Act
   c. 28-hour day
   d. Mass production

47. _____ was a Scottish moral philosopher and a pioneer of political economy. One of the key figures of the Scottish Enlightenment, Smith is the author of The Theory of Moral Sentiments and An Inquiry into the Nature and Causes of the Wealth of Nations. The latter, usually abbreviated as The Wealth of Nations, is considered his magnum opus and the first modern work of economics.
   a. Affirmative action
   b. Abraham Harold Maslow
   c. Adam Smith
   d. Affiliation

48. _____ Movement refers to those researchers of organizational development who study the behavior of people in groups, in particular workplace groups. It originated in the 1920s' Hawthorne studies, which examined the effects of social relations, motivation and employee satisfaction on factory productivity. The movement viewed workers in terms of their psychology and fit with companies, rather than as interchangeable parts.
   a. Hersey-Blanchard situational theory
   b. Work design
   c. Participatory management
   d. Human relations

49. _____ refers to those researchers of organizational development who study the behavior of people in groups, in particular workplace groups. It originated in the 1920s' Hawthorne studies, which examined the effects of social relations, motivation and employee satisfaction on factory productivity. The movement viewed workers in terms of their psychology and fit with companies, rather than as interchangeable parts.
   a. Job satisfaction
   b. Job analysis
   c. Path-goal theory
   d. Human relations movement

50. _____ and Theory Y are theories of human motivation created and developed by Douglas McGregor at the MIT Sloan School of Management in the 1960s that have been used in human resource management, organizational behavior, organizational communication and organizational development. They describe two very different attitudes toward workforce motivation. McGregor felt that companies followed either one or the other approach.

Chapter 1. Introduction to Operations Management

In _____, which many managers practice, management assumes employees are inherently lazy and will avoid work if they can. They inherently dislike work. Because of this, workers need to be closely supervised and comprehensive systems of controls developed.

a. Cash cow
b. Theory X
c. Management team
d. Job enrichment

51. In organizational development (OD), _____ is the application of Socio-Technical Systems principles and techniques to the humanization of work.

The aims of _____ to improved job satisfaction, to improved through-put, to improved quality and to reduced employee problems, e.g., grievances, absenteeism.

Under scientific management people would be directed by reason and the problems of industrial unrest would be appropriately (i.e., scientifically) addressed.

a. Graduate recruitment
b. Management process
c. Path-goal theory
d. Work design

52. The term '_____' refers to the concept of collecting information and attempting to spot a pattern in the information. In some fields of study, the term '_____' has more formally-defined meanings.

In project management _____ is a mathematical technique that uses historical results to predict future outcome.

a. Stepwise regression
b. Regression analysis
c. Trend analysis
d. Least squares

53. _____ is a concept that aims to enhance supply chain integration by supporting and assisting joint practices. _____ seeks cooperative management of inventory through joint visibility and replenishment of products throughout the supply chain. Information shared between suppliers and retailers aids in planning and satisfying customer demands through a supportive system of shared information.

a. Groups decision making
b. Collaborative Planning, Forecasting and Replenishment
c. Timesheets
d. Career portfolios

54. _____, commonly referred to as 'eBusiness' or 'e-Business', may be defined as the utilization of information and communication technologies (ICT) in support of all the activities of business. Commerce constitutes the exchange of products and services between businesses, groups and individuals and hence can be seen as one of the essential activities of any business. Hence, electronic commerce or eCommerce focuses on the use of ICT to enable the external activities and relationships of the business with individuals, groups and other businesses.

a. Electronic business
b. A Stake in the Outcome
c. A4e
d. AAAI

55. _____, commonly known as e-commerce, consists of the buying and selling of products or services over electronic systems such as the Internet and other computer networks. The amount of trade conducted electronically has grown extraordinarily with widespread Internet usage. The use of commerce is conducted in this way, spurring and drawing on innovations in electronic funds transfer, supply chain management, Internet marketing, online transaction processing, electronic data interchange (EDI), inventory management systems, and automated data collection systems.
   a. A Stake in the Outcome
   b. Online shopping
   c. A4e
   d. Electronic Commerce

56. _____ is a type of trade policy that allows traders to act and transact without interference from government. Thus, the policy permits trading partners mutual gains from trade, with goods and services produced according to the theory of comparative advantage.

Under a _____ policy, prices are a reflection of true supply and demand, and are the sole determinant of resource allocation.

   a. 33 Strategies of War
   b. 28-hour day
   c. 1990 Clean Air Act
   d. Free Trade

57. _____ is a designated group of countries that have agreed to eliminate tariffs, quotas and preferences on most (if not all) goods and services traded between them. It can be considered the second stage of economic integration. Countries choose this kind of economic integration form if their economical structures are complementary.
   a. 33 Strategies of War
   b. 28-hour day
   c. Free trade area
   d. 1990 Clean Air Act

58. The _____ was the outcome of the failure of negotiating governments to create the International Trade Organization (ITO.) GATT was formed in 1947 and lasted until 1994, when it was replaced by the World Trade Organization. The Bretton Woods Conference had introduced the idea for an organization to regulate trade as part of a larger plan for economic recovery after World War II.
   a. 1990 Clean Air Act
   b. Multilateral treaty
   c. 28-hour day
   d. General Agreement on Tariffs and Trade

59. The _____ is a trilateral trade bloc in North America created by the governments of the United States, Canada, and Mexico. The agreement creating the trade bloc came into force on January 1, 1994. It superseded the Canada-United States Free Trade Agreement between the U.S. and Canada.
   a. Career portfolios
   b. Trade union
   c. Business war game
   d. North American Free Trade Agreement

60. The phrase mergers and _____s refers to the aspect of corporate strategy, corporate finance and management dealing with the buying, selling and combining of different companies that can aid, finance, or help a growing company in a given industry grow rapidly without having to create another business entity.

An _____, also known as a takeover or a buyout, is the buying of one company (the 'target') by another. An _____ may be friendly or hostile.

a. Acquisition
b. AAAI
c. A4e
d. A Stake in the Outcome

61. _____ is subcontracting a process, such as product design or manufacturing, to a third-party company. The decision to outsource is often made in the interest of lowering cost or making better use of time and energy costs, redirecting or conserving energy directed at the competencies of a particular business, or to make more efficient use of land, labor, capital, (information) technology and resources. _____ became part of the business lexicon during the 1980s.
   a. Outsourcing
   b. Unemployment insurance
   c. Opinion leadership
   d. Operant conditioning

62. A _____ is the system of organizations, people, technology, activities, information and resources involved in moving a product or service from supplier to customer. _____ activities transform natural resources, raw materials and components into a finished product that is delivered to the end customer. In sophisticated _____ systems, used products may re-enter the _____ at any point where residual value is recyclable.
   a. Packaging
   b. Drop shipping
   c. Wholesalers
   d. Supply chain

63. _____, a business term, is a measure of how products and services supplied by a company meet or surpass customer expectation. It is seen as a key performance indicator within business and is part of the four perspectives of a Balanced Scorecard.

In a competitive marketplace where businesses compete for customers, _____ is seen as a key differentiator and increasingly has become a key element of business strategy.

   a. Critical Success Factor
   b. Horizontal integration
   c. Customer satisfaction
   d. Foreign ownership

64. The _____ is a combinatorial optimization algorithm which solves the assignment problem in polynomial time and which anticipated later primal-dual methods. It was developed and published by Harold Kuhn in 1955, who gave the name '_____' because the algorithm was largely based on the earlier works of two Hungarian mathematicians: D>énes KÅ'nig and JenÅ' Egerv>áry.

James Munkres reviewed the algorithm in 1957 and observed that it is (strongly) polynomial.

   a. 1990 Clean Air Act
   b. 33 Strategies of War
   c. 28-hour day
   d. Hungarian method

65. _____ is a Japanese philosophy that focuses on continuous improvement throughout all aspects of life. When applied to the workplace, _____ activities continually improve all functions of a business, from manufacturing to management and from the CEO to the assembly line workers. By improving standardized activities and processes, _____ aims to eliminate waste .
   a. Sensitivity analysis
   b. Kaizen
   c. Psychological pricing
   d. Cross-docking

Chapter 1. Introduction to Operations Management

66. In organizational development (OD), _____ is a series of actions taken by a Process Owner to identify, analyze and improve existing processes within an organization to meet new goals and objectives. These actions often follow a specific methodology or strategy to create successful results. A sampling of these are listed below.

a. Product innovation
b. Letter of resignation
c. Supervisory board
d. Process improvement

67. _____ is the process of understanding, anticipating and influencing consumer behavior in order to maximize revenue or profits from a fixed, perishable resource This process was first discovered by Dr. Matt H. Keller. The challenge is to sell the right resources to the right customer at the right time for the right price.

a. Gap analysis
b. Yield management
c. Business model design
d. Business networking

68. _____ is a business management strategy, initially implemented by Motorola, that today enjoys widespread application in many sectors of industry.

_____ seeks to improve the quality of process outputs by identifying and removing the causes of defects (errors) and variation in manufacturing and business processes. It uses a set of quality management methods, including statistical methods, and creates a special infrastructure of people within the organization ('Black Belts' etc.)

a. Six sigma
b. Takt time
c. Theory of constraints
d. Production line

69. _____ is a business management strategy aimed at embedding awareness of quality in all organizational processes. _____ has been widely used in manufacturing, education, hospitals, call centers, government, and service industries, as well as NASA space and science programs.

As defined by the International Organization for Standardization (ISO):

' _____ is a management approach for an organization, centered on quality, based on the participation of all its members and aiming at long-term success through customer satisfaction, and benefits to all members of the organization and to society.' ISO 8402:1994

One major aim is to reduce variation from every process so that greater consistency of effort is obtained. (Royse, D., Thyer, B., Padgett D., ' Logan T., 2006)

a. Quality management
b. Total quality management
c. 1990 Clean Air Act
d. 28-hour day

70. _____ can be considered to have three main components: quality control, quality assurance and quality improvement. _____ is focused not only on product quality, but also the means to achieve it. _____ therefore uses quality assurance and control of processes as well as products to achieve more consistent quality.

a. 1990 Clean Air Act
b. 28-hour day
c. Total quality management
d. Quality management

71. _____ is an effective method of monitoring a process through the use of control charts. Control charts enable the use of objective criteria for distinguishing background variation from events of significance based on statistical techniques. Much of its power lies in the ability to monitor both process center and its variation about that center.
   a. Statistical process control
   b. Process capability
   c. Single Minute Exchange of Die
   d. Quality control

72. _____ is the area of law in which manufacturers, distributors, suppliers, retailers, and others who make products available to the public are held responsible for the injuries those products cause.

In the United States, the claims most commonly associated with _____ are negligence, strict liability, breach of warranty, and various consumer protection claims. The majority of _____ laws are determined at the state level and vary widely from state to state.

   a. Product liability
   b. Right-to-work laws
   c. Railway Labor Act
   d. Leave of absence

Chapter 2. Competitiveness, Strategy, and Productivity

1. _____ is a form of communication that typically attempts to persuade potential customers to purchase or to consume more of a particular brand of product or service. 'While now central to the contemporary global economy and the reproduction of global production networks, it is only quite recently that _____ has been more than a marginal influence on patterns of sales and production. The formation of modern _____ was intimately bound up with the emergence of new forms of monopoly capitalism around the end of the 19th and beginning of the 20th century as one element in corporate strategies to create, organize and where possible control markets, especially for mass produced consumer goods.

   a. AAAI
   b. A Stake in the Outcome
   c. A4e
   d. Advertising

2. In economics, business, retail, and accounting, a _____ is the value of money that has been used up to produce something, and hence is not available for use anymore. In economics, a _____ is an alternative that is given up as a result of a decision. In business, the _____ may be one of acquisition, in which case the amount of money expended to acquire it is counted as _____.

   a. Cost overrun
   b. Fixed costs
   c. Cost allocation
   d. Cost

3. _____ is an integrated communications-based process through which individuals and communities discover that existing and newly-identified needs and wants may be satisfied by the products and services of others.

   _____ is defined by the American _____ Association as the activity, set of institutions, and processes for creating, communicating, delivering, and exchanging offerings that have value for customers, clients, partners, and society at large. The term developed from the original meaning which referred literally to going to market, as in shopping, or going to a market to buy or sell goods or services.

   a. Customer relationship management
   b. Market development
   c. Disruptive technology
   d. Marketing

4. _____ is an area of business concerned with the production of goods and services, and involves the responsibility of ensuring that business operations are efficient in terms of using as little resource as needed, and effective in terms of meeting customer requirements. It is concerned with managing the process that converts inputs (in the forms of materials, labour and energy) into outputs (in the form of goods and services.)

   Operations traditionally refers to the production of goods and services separately, although the distinction between these two main types of operations is increasingly difficult to make as manufacturers tend to merge product and service offerings.

   a. Operations management
   b. AAAI
   c. A Stake in the Outcome
   d. A4e

5. _____ is subcontracting a process, such as product design or manufacturing, to a third-party company. The decision to outsource is often made in the interest of lowering cost or making better use of time and energy costs, redirecting or conserving energy directed at the competencies of a particular business, or to make more efficient use of land, labor, capital, (information) technology and resources. _____ became part of the business lexicon during the 1980s.

   a. Operant conditioning
   b. Unemployment insurance
   c. Opinion leadership
   d. Outsourcing

6. _____ is one of the four Ps of the marketing mix. The other three aspects are product, promotion, and place. It is also a key variable in microeconomic price allocation theory.
   a. Penetration pricing
   b. Transfer pricing
   c. Price floor
   d. Pricing

7. _____ refers to metrics and measures of output from production processes, per unit of input. Labor _____, for example, is typically measured as a ratio of output per labor-hour, an input. _____ may be conceived of as a metrics of the technical or engineering efficiency of production.
   a. Master production schedule
   b. Remanufacturing
   c. Value engineering
   d. Productivity

8. _____ is a term defined by the Oxford English Dictionary as an individual's 'course or progress through life '. It is usually considered to pertain to remunerative work (and sometimes also formal education.)

The etymology of the term is somewhat ironic in that it comes from the Latin word carrera, which means race .

   a. Nursing shortage
   b. Career
   c. Career planning
   d. Spatial mismatch

9. _____ is the provision of service to customers before, during and after a purchase.

According to Turban et al. (2002), '_____ is a series of activities designed to enhance the level of customer satisfaction - that is, the feeling that a product or service has met the customer expectation.'

Its importance varies by product, industry and customer; defective or broken merchandise can be exchanged, often only with a receipt and within a specified time frame.

   a. Customer service
   b. Service rate
   c. 28-hour day
   d. 1990 Clean Air Act

10. _____ is an advertisement in which a particular product specifically mentions a competitor by name for the express purpose of showing why the competitor is inferior to the product naming it.

This should not be confused with parody advertisements, where a fictional product is being advertised for the purpose of poking fun at the particular advertisement, nor should it be confused with the use of a coined brand name for the purpose of comparing the product without actually naming an actual competitor. ('Wikipedia tastes better and is less filling than the Encyclopedia Galactica.')

In the 1980s, during what has been referred to as the cola wars, soft-drink manufacturer Pepsi ran a series of advertisements where people, caught on hidden camera, in a blind taste test, chose Pepsi over rival Coca-Cola.

   a. 28-hour day
   b. Comparative advertising
   c. 33 Strategies of War
   d. 1990 Clean Air Act

Chapter 2. Competitiveness, Strategy, and Productivity

11. A _____ is a brief written statement of the purpose of a company or organization. Ideally, a _____ guides the actions of the organization, spells out its overall goal, provides a sense of direction, and guides decision making for all levels of management.

_____s often contain the following:

- Purpose and aim of the organization
- The organization's primary stakeholders: clients, stockholders, etc.
- Responsibilities of the organization toward these stakeholders
- Products and services offered

In developing a _____:

- Encourage as much input as feasible from employees, volunteers, and other stakeholders
- Publicize it broadly

The _____ can be used to resolve differences between business stakeholders. Stakeholders include: employees including managers and executives, stockholders, board of directors, customers, suppliers, distributors, creditors, governments (local, state, federal, etc.), unions, competitors, NGO's, and the general public.

a. 1990 Clean Air Act
b. 33 Strategies of War
c. 28-hour day
d. Mission statement

12. _____ can be regarded as an outcome of mental processes (cognitive process) leading to the selection of a course of action among several alternatives. Every _____ process produces a final choice. The output can be an action or an opinion of choice.

a. 1990 Clean Air Act
b. 28-hour day
c. Decision making
d. 33 Strategies of War

13. A _____ structured in a way such that every entity in the organization, except one, is subordinate to a single other entity. This is the dominant mode of organization among large organizations; most corporations, governments, and organized religions are _____s. Hierarchies denote a singular/group of power at the top, a number of assistants underneath and hundreds of servants beneath them.

a. Matrix management
b. Catfish effect
c. CPS Model
d. Hierarchical organization

14. _____ is the process of determining the production capacity needed by an organization to meet changing demands for its products. In the context of _____, 'capacity' is the maximum amount of work that an organization is capable of completing in a given period of time.

A discrepancy between the capacity of an organization and the demands of its customers results in inefficiency, either in under-utilized resources or unfulfilled customers.

a. Productivity
b. Remanufacturing
c. Scientific management
d. Capacity planning

15. _____ is an inventory strategy that strives to improve the return on investment of a business by reducing in-process inventory and its associated carrying costs. To meet _____ objectives, the process relies on signals between different points in the process. This means the process is often driven by a series of signals, or Kanban, which tell production when to make the next part. Kanban are usually 'tickets' but can be simple visual signals, such as the presence or absence of a part on a shelf. Implemented correctly, _____ can dramatically improve a manufacturing organization's return on investment, quality, and efficiency.

a. 28-hour day
b. 33 Strategies of War
c. 1990 Clean Air Act
d. Just-in-time

16. _____ is a process of gathering, analyzing, and dispensing information for tactical or strategic purposes. The _____ process entails obtaining both factual and subjective information on the business environments in which a company is operating or considering entering.

There are three ways of scanning the business environment:

- Ad-hoc scanning - Short term, infrequent examinations usually initiated by a crisis
- Regular scanning - Studies done on a regular schedule (say, once a year)
- Continuous scanning(also called continuous learning) - continuous structured data collection and processing on a broad range of environmental factors

Most commentators feel that in today's turbulent business environment the best scanning method available is continuous scanning. This allows the firm to :

-act quickly-take advantage of opportunities before competitors do-respond to environmental threats before significant damage is done

a. A Stake in the Outcome
b. A4e
c. Environmental scanning
d. AAAI

17. The phrase _____ refers to the aspect of corporate strategy, corporate finance and management dealing with the buying, selling and combining of different companies that can aid, finance, or help a growing company in a given industry grow rapidly without having to create another business entity.

An acquisition, also known as a takeover or a buyout, is the buying of one company (the 'target') by another. An acquisition may be friendly or hostile.

a. Mergers and acquisitions
b. 28-hour day
c. 33 Strategies of War
d. 1990 Clean Air Act

Chapter 2. Competitiveness, Strategy, and Productivity

18. _____ is a strategic planning method used to evaluate the Strengths, Weaknesses, Opportunities, and Threats involved in a project or in a business venture. It involves specifying the objective of the business venture or project and identifying the internal and external factors that are favorable and unfavorable to achieving that objective. The technique is credited to Albert Humphrey, who led a convention at Stanford University in the 1960s and 1970s using data from Fortune 500 companies.

a. Marketing
b. Market share
c. Corporate image
d. SWOT analysis

19. The phrase mergers and _____s refers to the aspect of corporate strategy, corporate finance and management dealing with the buying, selling and combining of different companies that can aid, finance, or help a growing company in a given industry grow rapidly without having to create another business entity.

An _____, also known as a takeover or a buyout, is the buying of one company (the 'target') by another. An _____ may be friendly or hostile.

a. Acquisition
b. A4e
c. AAAI
d. A Stake in the Outcome

20. _____ as defined in business terms is an organization's strategic guide to globalization. A sound _____ should address these questions: what must be (versus what is) the extent of market presence in the world's major markets? How to build the necessary global presence? What must be (versus what is) the optimal locations around the world for the various value chain activities? How to run global presence into global competitive advantage?

Academic research on _____ came of age during the 1980s, including work by Michael Porter and Christopher Bartlett ' Sumantra Ghoshal. Among the forces perceived to bring about the globalization of competition were convergence in economic systems and technological change, especially in information technology, that facilitated and required the coordination of a multinational firm's strategy on a worldwide scale.

a. 28-hour day
b. 1990 Clean Air Act
c. 33 Strategies of War
d. Global strategy

21. _____ in its literal sense is the process of transformation of local or regional phenomena into global ones. It can be described as a process by which the people of the world are unified into a single society and function together.

This process is a combination of economic, technological, sociocultural and political forces.

a. Cost Management
b. Globalization
c. Histogram
d. Collaborative Planning, Forecasting and Replenishment

22. _____ is a term applied to an organization that has created the processes, tools, and training to enable it to respond quickly to customer needs and market changes while still controlling costs and quality.

An enabling factor in becoming an agile manufacturer has been the development of manufacturing support technology that allows the marketers, the designers and the production personnel to share a common database of parts and products, to share data on production capacities and problems -- particularly where small initial problems may have larger downstream effects. It is a general proposition of manufacturing that the cost of correcting quality issues increases as the problem moves downstream, so that it is cheaper to correct quality problems at the earliest possible point in the process.

a. A Stake in the Outcome
b. A4e
c. Agile manufacturing
d. AAAI

23. _____ is the amount of goods and services that a labourer produces in a given amount of time. It is one of several types of productivity that economists measure. _____ can be measured for a firm, a process or a country.
a. Business Network Transformation
b. Labour productivity
c. Time and attendance
d. Retroactive overtime

24. In economics and sociology, an _____ is any factor (financial or non-financial) that enables or motivates a particular course of action, or counts as a reason for preferring one choice to the alternatives. It is an expectation that encourages people to behave in a certain way. Since human beings are purposeful creatures, the study of _____ structures is central to the study of all economic activity (both in terms of individual decision-making and in terms of co-operation and competition within a larger institutional structure.)
a. AAAI
b. A Stake in the Outcome
c. Incentive
d. A4e

25. An _____ is a formal scheme used to promote or encourage specific actions or behavior by a specific group of people during a defined period of time. _____s are particularly used in business management to motivate employees, and in sales in order to attract and retain customers. The scientific literature also refers to this concept as Pay for Performance.
a. AAAI
b. A4e
c. A Stake in the Outcome
d. Incentive program

26. In a human resources context, _____ or labor _____ is the rate at which an employer gains and loses employees. Simple ways to describe it are 'how long employees tend to stay' or 'the rate of traffic through the revolving door.' _____ is measured for individual companies and for their industry as a whole. If an employer is said to have a high _____ relative to its competitors, it means that employees of that company have a shorter average tenure than those of other companies in the same industry.
a. Continuous
b. Career portfolios
c. Ten year occupational employment projection
d. Turnover

27. _____ is the temporary suspension or permanent termination of employment of an employee or (more commonly) a group of employees for business reasons, such as the decision that certain positions are no longer necessary or a business slow-down or interruption in work. Originally the term '_____' referred exclusively to a temporary interruption in work, as when factory work cyclically falls off. However, in recent times the term can also refer to the permanent elimination of a position.

a. Layoff
c. Wrongful dismissal
b. Termination of employment
d. Retirement

Chapter 3. Forecasting

1. _____ is the process of estimation in unknown situations. Prediction is a similar, but more general term. Both can refer to estimation of time series, cross-sectional or longitudinal data.
   - a. 28-hour day
   - b. 1990 Clean Air Act
   - c. 33 Strategies of War
   - d. Forecasting

2. The _____ is a systematic, interactive forecasting method which relies on a panel of independent experts. The carefully selected experts answer questionnaires in two or more rounds. After each round, a facilitator provides an anonymous summary of the experts' forecasts from the previous round as well as the reasons they provided for their judgments.
   - a. Hoshin Kanri
   - b. Delphi method
   - c. Learning organization
   - d. Quality function deployment

3. _____ is an increasingly broadening term with which an organization, or other human system describes the combination of traditionally administrative personnel functions with acquisition and application of skills, knowledge and experience, Employee Relations and resource planning at various levels. The field draws upon concepts developed in Industrial/Organizational Psychology and System Theory. _____ has at least two related interpretations depending on context. The original usage derives from political economy and economics, where it was traditionally called labor, one of four factors of production although this perspective is changing as a function of new and ongoing research into more strategic approaches at national levels. This first usage is used more in terms of '_____ development', and can go beyond just organizations to the level of nations . The more traditional usage within corporations and businesses refers to the individuals within a firm or agency, and to the portion of the organization that deals with hiring, firing, training, and other personnel issues, typically referred to as `_____ management'.
   - a. Human resource management
   - b. Human resources
   - c. Progressive discipline
   - d. Bradford Factor

4. The _____ is a combinatorial optimization algorithm which solves the assignment problem in polynomial time and which anticipated later primal-dual methods. It was developed and published by Harold Kuhn in 1955, who gave the name '_____' because the algorithm was largely based on the earlier works of two Hungarian mathematicians: D>énes KÅ'nig and JenÅ' Egerv>áry.

   James Munkres reviewed the algorithm in 1957 and observed that it is (strongly) polynomial.
   - a. 28-hour day
   - b. 1990 Clean Air Act
   - c. Hungarian method
   - d. 33 Strategies of War

5. _____ is an integrated communications-based process through which individuals and communities discover that existing and newly-identified needs and wants may be satisfied by the products and services of others.

   _____ is defined by the American _____ Association as the activity, set of institutions, and processes for creating, communicating, delivering, and exchanging offerings that have value for customers, clients, partners, and society at large. The term developed from the original meaning which referred literally to going to market, as in shopping, or going to a market to buy or sell goods or services.
   - a. Market development
   - b. Customer relationship management
   - c. Disruptive technology
   - d. Marketing

6. _____ is the process of understanding, anticipating and influencing consumer behavior in order to maximize revenue or profits from a fixed, perishable resource This process was first discovered by Dr. Matt H. Keller. The challenge is to sell the right resources to the right customer at the right time for the right price.

    a. Business networking   b. Gap analysis
    c. Yield management   d. Business model design

7. _____ is a form of communication that typically attempts to persuade potential customers to purchase or to consume more of a particular brand of product or service. 'While now central to the contemporary global economy and the reproduction of global production networks, it is only quite recently that _____ has been more than a marginal influence on patterns of sales and production. The formation of modern _____ was intimately bound up with the emergence of new forms of monopoly capitalism around the end of the 19th and beginning of the 20th century as one element in corporate strategies to create, organize and where possible control markets, especially for mass produced consumer goods.

    a. Advertising   b. AAAI
    c. A Stake in the Outcome   d. A4e

8. In economics, business, retail, and accounting, a _____ is the value of money that has been used up to produce something, and hence is not available for use anymore. In economics, a _____ is an alternative that is given up as a result of a decision. In business, the _____ may be one of acquisition, in which case the amount of money expended to acquire it is counted as _____.

    a. Cost overrun   b. Cost
    c. Cost allocation   d. Fixed costs

9. _____ can be regarded as an outcome of mental processes (cognitive process) leading to the selection of a course of action among several alternatives. Every _____ process produces a final choice. The output can be an action or an opinion of choice.

    a. 1990 Clean Air Act   b. Decision making
    c. 33 Strategies of War   d. 28-hour day

10. _____ is a broad label that refers to any individuals or households that use goods and services generated within the economy. The concept of a _____ is used in different contexts, so that the usage and significance of the term may vary.

Typically when business people and economists talk of _____s they are talking about person as _____, an aggregated commodity item with little individuality other than that expressed in the buy/not-buy decision.

    a. 1990 Clean Air Act   b. 28-hour day
    c. 33 Strategies of War   d. Consumer

11. _____ of the learning curve effect and the closely related experience curve effect express the relationship between equations for experience and efficiency or between efficiency gains and investment in the effort. The experience of 'learning curves' was first observed by the 19th Century German psychologist Hermann Ebbinghaus according to the difficulty of memorizing varying numbers of verbal stimuli, and subsequent learning about the complex processes of learning are discussed in the

The rule used for representing the learning curve effect states that the more times a task has been performed, the less time will be required on each subsequent iteration.

a. Distribution
b. Spatial Decision Support Systems
c. Point biserial correlation coefficient
d. Models

12. In statistics, signal processing, and many other fields, a _____ is a sequence of data points, measured typically at successive times, spaced at (often uniform) time intervals. _____ analysis comprises methods that attempt to understand such _____, often either to understand the underlying context of the data points (Where did they come from? What generated them?), or to make forecasts (predictions.) _____ forecasting is the use of a model to forecast future events based on known past events: to forecast future data points before they are measured.

a. Time series
b. Moving average
c. Standard deviation
d. Histogram

13. In statistics, many time series exhibit cyclic variation known as _____, periodic variation, or periodic fluctuations. This variation can be either regular or semiregular.

For example, retail sales tend to peak for the Christmas season and then decline after the holidays.

a. 1990 Clean Air Act
b. 33 Strategies of War
c. Seasonality
d. 28-hour day

14. The term '_____' refers to the concept of collecting information and attempting to spot a pattern in the information. In some fields of study, the term '_____' has more formally-defined meanings.

In project management _____ is a mathematical technique that uses historical results to predict future outcome.

a. Regression analysis
b. Least squares
c. Stepwise regression
d. Trend analysis

15. The phrase mergers and _____s refers to the aspect of corporate strategy, corporate finance and management dealing with the buying, selling and combining of different companies that can aid, finance, or help a growing company in a given industry grow rapidly without having to create another business entity.

An _____, also known as a takeover or a buyout, is the buying of one company (the 'target') by another. An _____ may be friendly or hostile.

a. A Stake in the Outcome
b. A4e
c. AAAI
d. Acquisition

16. In statistics, a _____ rolling mean or running average, is a type of finite impulse response filter used to analyze a set of data points by creating a series of averages of different subsets of the full data set. A _____ is not a single number, but it is a set of numbers, each of which is the average of the corresponding subset of a larger set of data points. A _____ may also use unequal weights for each data value in the subset to emphasize particular values in the subset.

a. Homoscedastic
c. Standard deviation
b. Time series analysis
d. Moving average

17. In statistics, _____ is a technique that can be applied to time series data, either to produce smoothed data for presentation, or to make forecasts. The time series data themselves are a sequence of observations. The observed phenomenon may be an essentially random process, or it may be an orderly, but noisy, process.

a. A Stake in the Outcome
c. Exponential smoothing
b. AAAI
d. A4e

18. In statistics and image processing, to smooth a data set is to create an approximating function that attempts to capture important patterns in the data, while leaving out noise or other fine-scale structures/rapid phenomena. Many different algorithms are used in _____. One of the most common algorithms is the 'moving average', often used to try to capture important trends in repeated statistical surveys.

a. 33 Strategies of War
c. 28-hour day
b. 1990 Clean Air Act
d. Smoothing

19. The term _____ usually refers to a weighted arithmetic mean, but weighted versions of other means can also be calculated, such as the weighted geometric mean and the weighted harmonic mean.

Given two school classes, one with 20 students, and one with 30 students, the grades in each class on a test were:

   Morning class = 62, 67, 71, 74, 76, 77, 78, 79, 79, 80, 80, 81, 81, 82, 83, 84, 86, 89, 93, 98

   Afternoon class = 81, 82, 83, 84, 85, 86, 87, 87, 88, 88, 89, 89, 89, 90, 90, 90, 90, 91, 91, 91, 92, 92, 93, 93, 94, 95, 96, 97, 98, 99

The straight average for the morning class is 80 and the straight average of the afternoon class is 90. The straight average of 80 and 90 is 85, the mean of the two class means.

a. 1990 Clean Air Act
c. 33 Strategies of War
b. Weighted average
d. 28-hour day

20. The method of _____ is used to approximately solve overdetermined systems, i.e. systems of equations in which there are more equations than unknowns. _____ is often applied in statistical contexts, particularly regression analysis.

_____ can be interpreted as a method of fitting data.

a. Trend analysis
c. Regression analysis
b. Stepwise regression
d. Least squares

21. In statistics, _____ is used for two things:

- to construct a simple formula that will predict a value or values for a variable given the value of another variable.
- to test whether and how a given variable is related to another variable or variables.

_____ is a form of regression analysis in which the relationship between one or more independent variables and another variable, called the dependent variable, is modelled by a least squares function, called a _____ equation. This function is a linear combination of one or more model parameters, called regression coefficients. A _____ equation with one independent variable represents a straight line when the predicted value (i.e. the dependent variable from the regression equation) is plotted against the independent variable: this is called a simple _____. However, note that 'linear' does not refer to this straight line, but rather to the way in which the regression coefficients occur in the regression equation.

a. Continuous
b. Clinical decision support systems
c. Strict liability
d. Linear regression

22. A _____ is a measure of the average price of consumer goods and services purchased by households. A _____ measures a price change for a constant market basket of goods and services from one period to the next within the same area (city, region, or nation.) It is a price index determined by measuring the price of a standard group of goods meant to represent the typical market basket of a typical urban consumer.

a. 1990 Clean Air Act
b. 33 Strategies of War
c. 28-hour day
d. Consumer price index

23. An _____ is a statistic about the economy. _____s allow analysis of economic performance and predictions of future performance.

_____s include various indices, earnings reports, and economic summaries, such as unemployment, housing starts, Consumer Price Index (a measure for inflation), industrial production, bankruptcies, Gross Domestic Product, broadband internet penetration, retail sales, stock market prices, and money supply changes.

a. AAAI
b. A4e
c. Economic indicator
d. A Stake in the Outcome

24. In statistics, _____ indicates the strength and direction of a linear relationship between two random variables. That is in contrast with the usage of the term in colloquial speech, which denotes any relationship, not necessarily linear. In general statistical usage, _____ or co-relation refers to the departure of two random variables from independence.

a. Correlation
b. Heteroskedastic
c. Time series analysis
d. Median

25. In the fields of science, engineering, industry and statistics, _____ is the degree of closeness of a measured or calculated quantity to its actual (true) value. _____ is closely related to precision, also called reproducibility or repeatability, the degree to which further measurements or calculations show the same or similar results. _____ indicates proximity to the true value, precision to the repeatability or reproducibility of the measurement

The results of calculations or a measurement can be accurate but not precise, precise but not accurate, neither, or both.

a. A4e
b. AAAI
c. Accuracy
d. A Stake in the Outcome

26. _____ is one of the managerial functions like planning, organizing, staffing and directing. It is an important function because it helps to check the errors and to take the corrective action so that deviation from standards are minimized and stated goals of the organization are achieved in desired manner. According to modern concepts, _____ is a foreseeing action whereas earlier concept of _____ was used only when errors were detected. _____ in management means setting standards, measuring actual performance and taking corrective action.

a. Control
b. Decision tree pruning
c. Turnover
d. Schedule of reinforcement

27. In statistics, _____ refers to techniques for the modeling and analysis of numerical data consisting of values of a dependent variable and of one or more independent variables The dependent variable in the regression equation is modeled as a function of the independent variables, corresponding parameters, and an error term. The error term is treated as a random variable and represents unexplained variation in the dependent variable.

a. Trend analysis
b. Stepwise regression
c. Regression Analysis
d. Least squares

28. _____ is measure of accuracy in a fitted time series value in statistics, specifically trending. It usually expresses accuracy as a percentage.

$$\text{MAPE} = \frac{1}{n}\sum_{t=1}^{n}\left|\frac{A_t - F_t}{A_t}\right|$$

The difference between actual value A_t and the forecast value F_t, is divided by the actual value A_t again.

a. Mean absolute percentage error
b. 1990 Clean Air Act
c. 33 Strategies of War
d. 28-hour day

29. In statistics, _____ is:

- the arithmetic _____
- the expected value of a random variable, which is also called the population _____.

It is sometimes stated that the '_____' _____s average. This is incorrect if '_____' is taken in the specific sense of 'arithmetic _____' as there are different types of averages: the _____, median, and mode. Other simple statistical analyses use measures of spread, such as range, interquartile range, or standard deviation. For a real-valued random variable X, the _____ is the expectation of X. Note that not every probability distribution has a defined _____; see the Cauchy distribution for an example.

a. Correlation
b. Statistical inference
c. Control chart
d. Mean

30. The _____ or simply average deviation of a data set is the average of the absolute deviations and is a summary statistic of statistical dispersion or variability. It is also called the mean absolute deviation, but this is easily confused with the median absolute deviation.

The average absolute deviation of a set $\{x_1, x_2, ..., x_n\}$ is

>

The choice of measure of central tendency, m(X), has a marked effect on the value of the average deviation.

a. AAAI
b. A4e
c. Average absolute deviation,
d. A Stake in the Outcome

31. In statistics, the _____ of an estimator is one of many ways to quantify the amount by which an estimator differs from the true value of the quantity being estimated. As a loss function, _____ is called squared error loss. _____ measures the average of the square of the 'error.' The error is the amount by which the estimator differs from the quantity to be estimated.

a. 1990 Clean Air Act
b. 28-hour day
c. 33 Strategies of War
d. Mean squared error

32. The _____ in statistical process control is a tool used to determine whether a manufacturing or business process is in a state of statistical control or not.

If the chart indicates that the process is currently under control then it can be used with confidence to predict the future performance of the process. If the chart indicates that the process being monitored is not in control, the pattern it reveals can help determine the source of variation to be eliminated to bring the process back into control.

a. Failure rate
b. Time series analysis
c. Simple moving average
d. Control chart

33. _____ is an effective method of monitoring a process through the use of control charts. Control charts enable the use of objective criteria for distinguishing background variation from events of significance based on statistical techniques. Much of its power lies in the ability to monitor both process center and its variation about that center.

a. Single Minute Exchange of Die
b. Process capability
c. Statistical process control
d. Quality control

34. In economics, _____ is the desire to own something and the ability to pay for it. The term _____ signifies the ability or the willingness to buy a particular commodity at a given point of time.

a. 33 Strategies of War
b. Demand
c. 1990 Clean Air Act
d. 28-hour day

35. _____ is an operational activity which does an aggregate plan for the production process, in advance of 2 to 18 months, to give an idea to management as to what quantity of materials and other resources are to be procured and when, so that the total cost of operations of the organization is kept to the minimum over that period.

The quantity of outsourcing, subcontracting of items, overtime of labor, numbers to be hired and fired in each period and the amount of inventory to be held in stock and to be backlogged for each period are decided. All of these activities are done within the framework of the company ethics, policies, and long term commitment to the society, community and the country of operation.

a. Earned value management
b. Earned Schedule
c. A Stake in the Outcome
d. Aggregate planning

Chapter 4. Product and Service Design

1. _____ is an advertisement in which a particular product specifically mentions a competitor by name for the express purpose of showing why the competitor is inferior to the product naming it.

This should not be confused with parody advertisements, where a fictional product is being advertised for the purpose of poking fun at the particular advertisement, nor should it be confused with the use of a coined brand name for the purpose of comparing the product without actually naming an actual competitor. ('Wikipedia tastes better and is less filling than the Encyclopedia Galactica.')

In the 1980s, during what has been referred to as the cola wars, soft-drink manufacturer Pepsi ran a series of advertisements where people, caught on hidden camera, in a blind taste test, chose Pepsi over rival Coca-Cola.

- a. 28-hour day
- b. Comparative advertising
- c. 1990 Clean Air Act
- d. 33 Strategies of War

2. A _____ is the belief that there is a technique, method, process, activity, incentive or reward that is more effective at delivering a particular outcome than any other technique, method, process, etc. The idea is that with proper processes, checks, and testing, a desired outcome can be delivered with fewer problems and unforeseen complications. _____s can also be defined as the most efficient (least amount of effort) and effective (best results) way of accomplishing a task, based on repeatable procedures that have proven themselves over time for large numbers of people.
- a. Fix it twice
- b. Best practice
- c. Hierarchical organization
- d. Design management

3. In economics, business, retail, and accounting, a _____ is the value of money that has been used up to produce something, and hence is not available for use anymore. In economics, a _____ is an alternative that is given up as a result of a decision. In business, the _____ may be one of acquisition, in which case the amount of money expended to acquire it is counted as _____.
- a. Fixed costs
- b. Cost allocation
- c. Cost overrun
- d. Cost

4. _____ is subcontracting a process, such as product design or manufacturing, to a third-party company. The decision to outsource is often made in the interest of lowering cost or making better use of time and energy costs, redirecting or conserving energy directed at the competencies of a particular business, or to make more efficient use of land, labor, capital, (information) technology and resources. _____ became part of the business lexicon during the 1980s.
- a. Opinion leadership
- b. Operant conditioning
- c. Unemployment insurance
- d. Outsourcing

5.

_____ is a systematic method to improve the 'value' of goods or products and services by using an examination of function. Value, as defined, is the ratio of function to cost. Value can therefore be increased by either improving the function or reducing the cost.

- a. Cellular manufacturing
- b. Master production schedule
- c. Capacity planning
- d. Value engineering

Chapter 4. Product and Service Design

6. _____, a business term, is a measure of how products and services supplied by a company meet or surpass customer expectation. It is seen as a key performance indicator within business and is part of the four perspectives of a Balanced Scorecard.

In a competitive marketplace where businesses compete for customers, _____ is seen as a key differentiator and increasingly has become a key element of business strategy.

- a. Foreign ownership
- b. Critical Success Factor
- c. Customer satisfaction
- d. Horizontal integration

7. A _____ is a relatively new executive level position at a corporation, company, organization typically reporting directly to the CEO or board of directors. The _____ is responsible for a brand's image, experience, and promise, and propagating it throughout all aspects of the company. The brand officer oversees marketing, advertising, design, public relations and customer service departments.

- a. Director of communications
- b. Purchasing manager
- c. Chief executive officer
- d. Chief brand officer

8. The _____ is an agency of the United States Department of Health and Human Services and is responsible for regulating and supervising the safety of foods, dietary supplements, drugs, vaccines, biological medical products, blood products, medical devices, radiation-emitting devices, veterinary products, and cosmetics. The FDA also enforces section 361 of the Public Health Service Act and the associated regulations, including sanitation requirements on interstate travel as well as specific rules for control of disease on products ranging from pet turtles to semen donations for assisted reproductive medicine techniques.

The FDA is an agency within the United States Department of Health and Human Services responsible for protecting and promoting the nation's public health.

- a. 1990 Clean Air Act
- b. Food and Drug Administration
- c. 28-hour day
- d. 33 Strategies of War

9. _____ is the area of law in which manufacturers, distributors, suppliers, retailers, and others who make products available to the public are held responsible for the injuries those products cause.

In the United States, the claims most commonly associated with _____ are negligence, strict liability, breach of warranty, and various consumer protection claims. The majority of _____ laws are determined at the state level and vary widely from state to state.

- a. Right-to-work laws
- b. Railway Labor Act
- c. Product liability
- d. Leave of absence

10. The _____, first published in 1952, is one of a number of uniform acts that have been promulgated in conjunction with efforts to harmonize the law of sales and other commercial transactions in all 50 states within the United States of America. This objective is deemed important because of the prevalence of commercial transactions that extend beyond one state (for example, where the goods are manufactured in state A, warehoused in state B, sold from state C and delivered in state D.) The _____ deals primarily with transactions involving personal property (movable property), not real property (immovable property.)

Chapter 4. Product and Service Design

a. A4e
b. AAAI
c. A Stake in the Outcome
d. Uniform Commercial Code

11. _____ can be regarded as an outcome of mental processes (cognitive process) leading to the selection of a course of action among several alternatives. Every _____ process produces a final choice. The output can be an action or an opinion of choice.
   a. 28-hour day
   b. 33 Strategies of War
   c. Decision making
   d. 1990 Clean Air Act

12. An _____ is the negative aspects of human activity on the biophysical environment. Environmentalism, a social and environmental movement that started in the 1960s, focuses on addressing _____s through advocacy, education and activism.

Major current _____s are climate change, pollution and resource depletion.

   a. AAAI
   b. A4e
   c. A Stake in the Outcome
   d. Environmental issue

13. In economics, _____ is the desire to own something and the ability to pay for it. The term _____ signifies the ability or the willingness to buy a particular commodity at a given point of time.
   a. 28-hour day
   b. 33 Strategies of War
   c. 1990 Clean Air Act
   d. Demand

14. _____ is an operational activity which does an aggregate plan for the production process, in advance of 2 to 18 months, to give an idea to management as to what quantity of materials and other resources are to be procured and when, so that the total cost of operations of the organization is kept to the minimum over that period.

The quantity of outsourcing, subcontracting of items, overtime of labor, numbers to be hired and fired in each period and the amount of inventory to be held in stock and to be backlogged for each period are decided. All of these activities are done within the framework of the company ethics, policies, and long term commitment to the society, community and the country of operation.

   a. A Stake in the Outcome
   b. Aggregate planning
   c. Earned value management
   d. Earned Schedule

15. _____ are parts that are for practical purposes identical. They are made to specifications that ensure that they are so nearly identical that they will fit into any device of the same type. One such part can freely replace another, without any custom fitting (such as filing.)
   a. Interchangeable parts
   b. A Stake in the Outcome
   c. A4e
   d. AAAI

16. _____ or Postponement is a concept in supply chain management where the manufacturing process starts by making a generic or family product that is later differentiated into a specific end-product. This is a widely used method, especially in industries with high demand uncertainty, and can be effectively used to address the final demand even if forecasts cannot be improved.

An example would be Benetton and their knitted sweaters that are initially all white, and then dyed into different colors only when the season/customer color preference/demand is known.

   a. Demand chain
   c. Delayed differentiation
   b. Supply-Chain Operations Reference
   d. Materials management

17. _____, in marketing, manufacturing, call centres and management, is the use of flexible computer-aided manufacturing systems to produce custom output. Those systems combine the low unit costs of mass production processes with the flexibility of individual customization.

'_____' is the new frontier in business competition for both manufacturing and service industries.

   a. 33 Strategies of War
   c. 1990 Clean Air Act
   b. Mass customization
   d. 28-hour day

18. In systems engineering, _____ is an approach that subdivides a system into smaller parts (modules) that can be independently created and then used in different systems to drive multiple functionalities. Besides reduction in cost (due to lesser customization, and less learning time), and flexibility in design, modularity offers other benefits such as augmentation (adding new solution by merely plugging in a new module), and exclusion. Examples of modular systems are cars, computers and high rise buildings.

   a. 28-hour day
   c. 1990 Clean Air Act
   b. Statement of work
   d. Modular design

19. _____ is the design of all information-gathering exercises where variation is present, whether under the full control of the experimenter or not. (The latter situation is usually called an observational study.) Often the experimenter is interested in the effect of some process or intervention (the 'treatment') on some objects (the 'experimental units'), which may be people, parts of people, groups of people, etc.

   a. Design of experiments
   c. 28-hour day
   b. Taguchi methods
   d. 1990 Clean Air Act

20. 'Speaking generally, properties are those physical quantities which directly describe the physical attributes of the system; _____s are those combinations of the properties which suffice to determine the response of the system. Properties can have all sorts of dimensions, depending upon the system being considered; _____s are dimensionless, or have the dimension of time or its reciprocal.'

The term can also be used in engineering contexts, however, as it is typically used in the physical sciences.

When the terms formal _____ and actual _____ are used, they generally correspond with the definitions used in computer science.

   a. Parameter
   c. 28-hour day
   b. 1990 Clean Air Act
   d. 33 Strategies of War

21. _____ in its literal sense is the process of transformation of local or regional phenomena into global ones. It can be described as a process by which the people of the world are unified into a single society and function together.

Chapter 4. Product and Service Design

This process is a combination of economic, technological, sociocultural and political forces.

a. Globalization
b. Collaborative Planning, Forecasting and Replenishment
c. Cost Management
d. Histogram

22. _____ can be defined as the idea generation, concept development, testing and manufacturing or implementation of a physical object or service. _____ers conceptualize and evaluate ideas, making them tangible through products in a more systematic approach. The role of a _____er encompasses many characteristics of the marketing manager, product manager, industrial designer and design engineer.

a. Affiliation
b. Adam Smith
c. Product design
d. Abraham Harold Maslow

23. _____ is the process of discovering the technological principles of a device, object or system through analysis of its structure, function and operation. It often involves taking something (e.g., a mechanical device, electronic component, or software program) apart and analyzing its workings in detail to be used in maintenance, or to try to make a new device or program that does the same thing without copying anything from the original.

_____ has its origins in the analysis of hardware for commercial or military advantage .

a. 1990 Clean Air Act
b. Reverse engineering
c. 28-hour day
d. Predictive maintenance

24. The phrase _____, according to the Organization for Economic Co-operation and Development, refers to 'creative work undertaken on a systematic basis in order to increase the stock of knowledge, including knowledge of man, culture and society, and the use of this stock of knowledge to devise new applications [sic]'

New product design and development is more than often a crucial factor in the survival of a company. In an industry that is fast changing, firms must continually revise their design and range of products. This is necessary due to continuous technology change and development as well as other competitors and the changing preference of customers.

a. 28-hour day
b. 1990 Clean Air Act
c. 33 Strategies of War
d. Research and development

25. _____ is a work methodology based on the parallelization of tasks (ie. concurrently.) It refers to an approach used in product development in which functions of design engineering, manufacturing engineering and other functions are integrated to reduce the elapsed time required to bring a new product to the market.

a. Concurrent engineering
b. Critical Chain Project Management
c. Work package
d. Project management

26. An _____ is a manufacturing process in which parts (usually interchangeable parts) are added to a product in a sequential manner using optimally planned logistics to create a finished product much faster than with handcrafting-type methods. The _____ developed by Ford Motor Company between 1908 and 1915 made _____s famous in the following decade through the social ramifications of mass production, such as the affordability of the Ford Model T and the introduction of high wages for Ford workers. However, the various preconditions for the development at Ford stretched far back into the 19th century, from the gradual realization of the dream of interchangeability, to the concept of reinventing workflow and job descriptions using analytical methods.

a. AAAI
b. A4e
c. A Stake in the Outcome
d. Assembly line

27. _____ is the process of disassembly and recovery at the module level and, eventually, at the component level. It requires the repair or replacement of worn out or obsolete components and modules. Parts subject to degradation affecting the performance or the expected life of the whole are replaced.

a. Productivity
b. Methods-time measurement
c. Capacity planning
d. Remanufacturing

28. _____ is a 'method to transform user demands into design quality, to deploy the functions forming quality, and to deploy methods for achieving the design quality into subsystems and component parts, and ultimately to specific elements of the manufacturing process.' , as described by Dr. Yoji Akao, who originally developed _____ in Japan in 1966, when the author combined his work in quality assurance and quality control points with function deployment used in Value Engineering.

_____ is designed to help planners focus on characteristics of a new or existing product or service from the viewpoints of market segments, company, or technology-development needs. The technique yields graphs and matrices.

a. Quality function deployment
b. 1990 Clean Air Act
c. Learning organization
d. Hoshin Kanri

29. _____ is a graphic tool for defining the relationship between customer desires and the firm/product capabilities. It is a part of the Quality Function Deployment (QFD) and it utilizes a planning matrix to relate what the customer wants to how a firm (that produce the products) is going to meet those wants. It looks like a House with correlation matrix as its roof, customer wants versus product features as the main part, competitor evaluation as the porch etc.

a. Decision Matrix
b. Health management system
c. Consensus-seeking decision-making
d. House of quality

30. _____ is the frequency with which an engineered system or component fails, expressed for example in failures per hour. It is often denoted by the Greek letter $>\lambda$ and is important in reliability theory.

The _____ of a system usually depends on time, with the rate varying over the life cycle of the system.

a. Heteroskedastic
b. Correlation
c. Statistics
d. Failure rate

Chapter 5. Strategic Capacity Planning for Products and Services

1. _____ is the process of determining the production capacity needed by an organization to meet changing demands for its products. In the context of _____, 'capacity' is the maximum amount of work that an organization is capable of completing in a given period of time.

A discrepancy between the capacity of an organization and the demands of its customers results in inefficiency, either in under-utilized resources or unfulfilled customers.

a. Scientific management
b. Productivity
c. Remanufacturing
d. Capacity planning

2. _____ is an operational activity which does an aggregate plan for the production process, in advance of 2 to 18 months, to give an idea to management as to what quantity of materials and other resources are to be procured and when, so that the total cost of operations of the organization is kept to the minimum over that period.

The quantity of outsourcing, subcontracting of items, overtime of labor, numbers to be hired and fired in each period and the amount of inventory to be held in stock and to be backlogged for each period are decided. All of these activities are done within the framework of the company ethics, policies, and long term commitment to the society, community and the country of operation.

a. Aggregate planning
b. Earned value management
c. A Stake in the Outcome
d. Earned Schedule

3. _____ is a concept in economics which refers to the extent to which an enterprise or a nation actually uses its installed productive capacity. Thus, it refers to the relationship between actual output that 'is' produced with the installed equipment and the potential output which 'could' be produced with it, if capacity was fully used.

If market demand grows, _____ will rise.

a. Multifactor productivity
b. Factors of production
c. Diseconomies of scale
d. Capacity utilization

4. _____s are the recurring expenses which are related to the operation of a business -- or to the operation of a device, component, piece of equipment or facility.

For a commercial enterprise, _____s fall into two broad categories:

- fixed costs, which are the same whether the operation is closed or running at 100% capacity
- variable costs, which may increase depending on whether more production is done, and how it is done (producing 100 items of product might require 10 days of normal time or take 7 days if overtime is used. It may be more or less expensive to use overtime production depending on whether faster production means the product can be more profitable.)

Overhead costs for a business are the cost of resources used by an organization just to maintain its existence. Overhead costs are usually measured in monetary terms, but non-monetary overhead is possible in the form of time required to accomplish tasks.

Examples of overhead costs include:

- payment of rent on the office space a business occupies
- cost of electricity for the office lights
- some office personnel wages

Non-overhead costs are incremental costs, such as the cost of raw materials used in the goods a business sells.

In the case of a device, component, piece of equipment or facility (for the rest of this article, all of these items will be referred to in general as equipment), it is the regular, usual and customary recurring costs of operating the equipment.

a. Intangible assets
b. Induction programme
c. Industrial market segmentation
d. Operating cost

5. In economics, business, retail, and accounting, a _____ is the value of money that has been used up to produce something, and hence is not available for use anymore. In economics, a _____ is an alternative that is given up as a result of a decision. In business, the _____ may be one of acquisition, in which case the amount of money expended to acquire it is counted as _____.

a. Cost allocation
b. Cost overrun
c. Cost
d. Fixed costs

6. _____ in its literal sense is the process of transformation of local or regional phenomena into global ones. It can be described as a process by which the people of the world are unified into a single society and function together.

This process is a combination of economic, technological, sociocultural and political forces.

a. Cost Management
b. Globalization
c. Collaborative Planning, Forecasting and Replenishment
d. Histogram

7. In queueing theory, _____ is the proportion of the system's resources which is used by the traffic which arrives at it. It should be strictly less than one for the system to function well. It is usually represented by the symbol ρ.

a. AAAI
b. Utilization
c. A4e
d. A Stake in the Outcome

8. The _____ is a combinatorial optimization algorithm which solves the assignment problem in polynomial time and which anticipated later primal-dual methods. It was developed and published by Harold Kuhn in 1955, who gave the name '_____' because the algorithm was largely based on the earlier works of two Hungarian mathematicians: D>énes KÅ'nig and JenÅ' Egerv>áry.

James Munkres reviewed the algorithm in 1957 and observed that it is (strongly) polynomial.

Chapter 5. Strategic Capacity Planning for Products and Services

a. 28-hour day
b. Hungarian method
c. 33 Strategies of War
d. 1990 Clean Air Act

9. A _____ is the system of organizations, people, technology, activities, information and resources involved in moving a product or service from supplier to customer. _____ activities transform natural resources, raw materials and components into a finished product that is delivered to the end customer. In sophisticated _____ systems, used products may re-enter the _____ at any point where residual value is recyclable.
a. Packaging
b. Drop shipping
c. Wholesalers
d. Supply chain

10. The _____ is a systematic, interactive forecasting method which relies on a panel of independent experts. The carefully selected experts answer questionnaires in two or more rounds. After each round, a facilitator provides an anonymous summary of the experts' forecasts from the previous round as well as the reasons they provided for their judgments.
a. Hoshin Kanri
b. Quality function deployment
c. Delphi method
d. Learning organization

11. In economics, _____ is the desire to own something and the ability to pay for it. The term _____ signifies the ability or the willingness to buy a particular commodity at a given point of time.
a. 1990 Clean Air Act
b. Demand
c. 33 Strategies of War
d. 28-hour day

12. _____ is the process of estimation in unknown situations. Prediction is a similar, but more general term. Both can refer to estimation of time series, cross-sectional or longitudinal data.
a. 1990 Clean Air Act
b. 28-hour day
c. 33 Strategies of War
d. Forecasting

13. In statistics, signal processing, and many other fields, a _____ is a sequence of data points, measured typically at successive times, spaced at (often uniform) time intervals. _____ analysis comprises methods that attempt to understand such _____, often either to understand the underlying context of the data points (Where did they come from? What generated them?), or to make forecasts (predictions.) _____ forecasting is the use of a model to forecast future events based on known past events: to forecast future data points before they are measured.
a. Histogram
b. Moving average
c. Standard deviation
d. Time series

14. In statistics, many time series exhibit cyclic variation known as _____, periodic variation, or periodic fluctuations. This variation can be either regular or semiregular.

For example, retail sales tend to peak for the Christmas season and then decline after the holidays.

a. Seasonality
b. 1990 Clean Air Act
c. 33 Strategies of War
d. 28-hour day

15. _____ is an advertisement in which a particular product specifically mentions a competitor by name for the express purpose of showing why the competitor is inferior to the product naming it.

This should not be confused with parody advertisements, where a fictional product is being advertised for the purpose of poking fun at the particular advertisement, nor should it be confused with the use of a coined brand name for the purpose of comparing the product without actually naming an actual competitor. ('Wikipedia tastes better and is less filling than the Encyclopedia Galactica.')

In the 1980s, during what has been referred to as the cola wars, soft-drink manufacturer Pepsi ran a series of advertisements where people, caught on hidden camera, in a blind taste test, chose Pepsi over rival Coca-Cola.

a. 1990 Clean Air Act
b. 28-hour day
c. 33 Strategies of War
d. Comparative advertising

16. In economics, _____ are business expenses that are not dependent on the activities of the business They tend to be time-related, such as salaries or rents being paid per month. This is in contrast to variable costs, which are volume-related (and are paid per quantity.)

In management accounting, _____ are defined as expenses that do not change in proportion to the activity of a business, within the relevant period or scale of production.

a. Cost allocation
b. Fixed costs
c. Cost of quality
d. Transaction cost

17. _____ is subcontracting a process, such as product design or manufacturing, to a third-party company. The decision to outsource is often made in the interest of lowering cost or making better use of time and energy costs, redirecting or conserving energy directed at the competencies of a particular business, or to make more efficient use of land, labor, capital, (information) technology and resources. _____ became part of the business lexicon during the 1980s.

a. Opinion leadership
b. Unemployment insurance
c. Operant conditioning
d. Outsourcing

18. In decision theory and estimation theory, the _____ of an estimator, $\hat{\theta}$, of an unknown parameter of the distribution, θ, is the expected value of the loss function

$$R(\theta, \hat{\theta}) = \mathbb{E}_\theta L(\theta, \hat{\theta}) = \int L(\theta, \hat{\theta})\, dP_\theta.$$

Chapter 5. Strategic Capacity Planning for Products and Services

where dP_θ is a probability measure parametrized by θ.

- For a scalar parameter θ and a quadratic loss function,

$$L(\theta, \hat{\theta}) = (\theta - \hat{\theta})^2$$

the _____ function becomes the mean squared error of the estimate,

$$R(\theta, \hat{\theta}) = E_\theta(\theta - \hat{\theta})^2$$

- In density estimation, the unknown parameter is probability density itself. The loss function is typically chosen to be a norm in an appropriate function space. For example, for L^2 norm,

$$L(f, \hat{f}) = \|f - \hat{f}\|_2^2$$

the _____ function becomes the mean integrated squared error

$$R(f, \hat{f}) = E\|f - \hat{f}\|^2$$

a. Linear model
c. Financial modeling
b. Risk aversion
d. Risk

19. _____ can be regarded as an outcome of mental processes (cognitive process) leading to the selection of a course of action among several alternatives. Every _____ process produces a final choice. The output can be an action or an opinion of choice.
    a. 1990 Clean Air Act
    b. 28-hour day
    c. Decision making
    d. 33 Strategies of War

20. _____, in microeconomics, are the cost advantages that a business obtains due to expansion. They are factors that cause a producer's average cost per unit to fall as scale is increased. _____ is a long run concept and refers to reductions in unit cost as the size of a facility, or scale, increases.
    a. A4e
    b. Economies of scope
    c. Economies of scale
    d. A Stake in the Outcome

21. _____ are the forces that cause larger firms to produce goods and services at increased per-unit costs. They are less well known than what economists have long understood as 'economies of scale', the forces which enable larger firms to produce goods and services at reduced per-unit costs.

Some of the forces which cause a diseconomy of scale are listed below:

Ideally, all employees of a firm would have one-on-one communication with each other so they know exactly what the other workers are doing.

- a. Factors of production
- b. Diseconomies of scale
- c. Production function
- d. Multifactor productivity

22. _____ is one of the four elements of marketing mix. An organization or set of organizations (go-betweens) involved in the process of making a product or service available for use or consumption by a consumer or business user.

The other three parts of the marketing mix are product, pricing, and promotion.

- a. Matching theory
- b. Distribution
- c. Job creation programs
- d. Missing completely at random

23. _____s are expenses that change in proportion to the activity of a business. In other words, _____ is the sum of marginal costs. It can also be considered normal costs.

- a. Variable cost
- b. Cost overrun
- c. Cost accounting
- d. Fixed costs

24. In economics ' business, specifically cost accounting, the _____ is the point at which cost or expenses and revenue are equal: there is no net loss or gain, and one has 'broken even'. A profit or a loss has not been made, although opportunity costs have been paid, and capital has received the risk-adjusted, expected return.

For example, if the business sells less than 200 tables each month, it will make a loss, if it sells more, it will be a profit.

- a. Fixed asset turnover
- b. Virtuous circle
- c. Defined benefit pension plan
- d. Break-even point

25. In cost-volume-profit analysis, a form of management accounting, _____ is the marginal profit per unit sale. It is a useful quantity in carrying out various calculations, and can be used as a measure of operating leverage.

The Total _____ is Total Revenue (TR, or Sales) minus Total Variable Cost (TVC):

TContribution margin = TR − TVC

The Unit _____ (C) is Unit Revenue (Price, P) minus Unit Variable Cost (V):

C = P − V

The _____ Ratio is the percentage of Contribution over Total Revenue, which can be calculated from the unit contribution over unit price or total contribution over Total Revenue:

$$\frac{C}{P} = \frac{P-V}{P} = \frac{\text{Unit Contribution Margin}}{\text{Price}} = \frac{\text{Total Contribution Margin}}{\text{Total Revenue}}$$

For instance, if the price is $10 and the unit variable cost is $2, then the unit _____ is $8, and the _____ ratio is $8/$10 = 80%.

a. Customer profitability
b. Profit center
c. Factory overhead
d. Contribution margin

26. _____ refers to the movement of cash into or out of a business or financial product. It is usually measured during a specified, finite period of time. Measurement of _____ can be used

- to determine a project's rate of return or value. The time of _____s into and out of projects are used as inputs in financial models such as internal rate of return, and net present value.
- to determine problems with a business's liquidity. Being profitable does not necessarily mean being liquid. A company can fail because of a shortage of cash, even while profitable.
- as an alternate measure of a business's profits when it is believed that accrual accounting concepts do not represent economic realities. For example, a company may be notionally profitable but generating little operational cash (as may be the case for a company that barters its products rather than selling for cash.) In such a case, the company may be deriving additional operating cash by issuing shares evaluating default risk, re-investment requirements, etc.

_____ is a generic term used differently depending on the context. It may be defined by users for their own purposes.

a. Sweat equity
b. Cash flow
c. Gross profit margin
d. Gross profit

27. _____ in mathematics and statistics is concerned with identifying the values, uncertainties and other issues relevant in a given decision and the resulting optimal decision. It is sometimes called game theory.

Most of _____ is normative or prescriptive, i.e., it is concerned with identifying the best decision to take, assuming an ideal decision maker who is fully informed, able to compute with perfect accuracy, and fully rational.

a. Nominal group technique
b. Rational planning model
c. Belief decision matrix
d. Decision theory

28. _____ refers to an assessment of the viability, stability and profitability of a business, sub-business or project.

It is performed by professionals who prepare reports using ratios that make use of information taken from financial statements and other reports. These reports are usually presented to top management as one of their bases in making business decisions.

Chapter 5. Strategic Capacity Planning for Products and Services

a. 33 Strategies of War
b. 28-hour day
c. 1990 Clean Air Act
d. Financial analysis

29. The _____ is a rate of return used in capital budgeting to measure and compare the profitability of investments. It is also called the discounted cash flow rate of return (DCFROR) or simply the rate of return (ROR.) In the context of savings and loans the IRR is also called the effective interest rate.
    a. AAAI
    b. A4e
    c. A Stake in the Outcome
    d. Internal rate of return

30. _____ is the value on a given date of a future payment or series of future payments, discounted to reflect the time value of money and other factors such as investment risk. _____ calculations are widely used in business and economics to provide a means to compare cash flows at different times on a meaningful 'like to like' basis.

    If offered a choice between $100 today or $100 in one year, everyone will choose $100 today.

    a. Net present value
    b. Discounted cash flow
    c. 1990 Clean Air Act
    d. Present value

31. Simply put, _____ is the value of money figuring in a given amount of interest for a given amount of time. For example 100 dollars of today's money held for a year at 5 percent interest is worth 105 dollars, therefore 100 dollars paid now or 105 dollars paid exactly one year from now is the same amount of payment of money with that given interest at that given amount of time. This notion dates at least to Martín de Azpilcueta of the School of Salamanca.
    a. Panjer recursion
    b. Time value of money
    c. Risk aversion
    d. Financial modeling

32. In finance, _____, is the ratio of money gained or lost on an investment relative to the amount of money invested. The amount of money gained or lost may be referred to as interest, profit/loss, gain/loss, or net income/loss. The money invested may be referred to as the asset, capital, principal, or the cost basis of the investment.
    a. Rate of return
    b. Return on Capital Employed
    c. Financial ratio
    d. Return on sales

33. _____ is a concept based on the fact that rationality of individuals is limited by the information they have, the cognitive limitations of their minds, and the finite amount of time they have to make decisions. This contrasts with the concept of rationality as optimization. Another way to look at _____ is that, because decision-makers lack the ability and resources to arrive at the optimal solution, they instead apply their rationality only after having greatly simplified the choices available.
    a. Mixed strategy
    b. Complete information
    c. Transferable utility
    d. Bounded rationality

34. _____ is an overall management philosophy introduced by Dr. Eliyahu M. Goldratt in his 1984 book titled The Goal, that is geared to help organizations continually achieve their goal. The title comes from the contention that any manageable system is limited in achieving more of its goal by a very small number of constraints, and that there is always at least one constraint. The _____ process seeks to identify the constraint and restructure the rest of the organization around it, through the use of the Five Focusing Steps.

a. Production line
c. Takt time
b. Six Sigma
d. Theory of constraints

35. In statistical decision theory, where we are faced with the problem of estimating a deterministic parameter (vector) $\theta \in \Theta$ from observations $x \in \mathcal{X}$, an estimator (estimation rule) δ^M is called _____ if its maximal risk is minimal among all estimators of θ. In a sense this means that δ^M is an estimator which performs best in the worst possible case allowed in the problem.

Consider the problem of estimating a deterministic (not Bayesian) parameter $\theta \in \Theta$ from noisy or corrupt data $x \in \mathcal{X}$ related through the conditional probability distribution $P(x|\theta)$.

a. Control
c. Battle Force Tactical Trainer
b. Backdating
d. Minimax

36. A _____ is a decision support tool that uses a tree-like graph or model of decisions and their possible consequences, including chance event outcomes, resource costs, and utility. _____s are commonly used in operations research, specifically in decision analysis, to help identify a strategy most likely to reach a goal. Another use of _____s is as a descriptive means for calculating conditional probabilities.

a. 1990 Clean Air Act
c. 28-hour day
b. 33 Strategies of War
d. Decision tree

37. In probability theory and statistics, the _____ of a random variable is the integral of the random variable with respect to its probability measure. For discrete random variables this is equivalent to the probability-weighted sum of the possible values, and for continuous random variables with a density function it is the probability density -weighted integral of the possible values.

a. AAAI
c. A Stake in the Outcome
b. A4e
d. Expected value

38. In decision theory, the _____ is the price that one would be willing to pay in order to gain access to perfect information.

The problem is modeled with a payoff matrix R_{ij} in which the row index i describes a choice that must be made by the payer, while the column index j describes a random variable that the payer does not yet have knowledge of, that has probability p_j of being in state j. If the payer is to choose i without knowing the value of j, the best choice is the one that maximizes the expected monetary value:

$$\mathrm{EMV} = \max_i \sum_j p_j R_{ij}.$$

where

$$\sum_j p_j R_{ij}.$$

is the expected payoff for action i i.e. the expectation value, and

$$EMV = \max_i$$

is choosing the maximum of these expectations for all available actions.

a. ELECTRE
b. Analytic Network Process
c. Expected value of perfect information
d. Ulysses pact

39. In game theory, a game is said to have _____ if all players know all moves that have taken place.

Chess is an example of a game with _____ as each player can see all of the pieces on the board at all times. Other examples of perfect games include tic tac toe, irensei and go.

In microeconomics, a state of _____ is assumed in some models of perfect competition. That is, assuming that all agents are rational and have _____, they will choose the best products, and the market will reward those who make the best products with higher sales.

a. Global games
b. Perfect information
c. Complete information
d. Transferable utility

40. In mathematics, _____ is a technique for optimization of a linear objective function, subject to linear equality and linear inequality constraints. Informally, _____ determines the way to achieve the best outcome (such as maximum profit or lowest cost) in a given mathematical model and given some list of requirements represented as linear equations.

More formally, given a polytope (for example, a polygon or a polyhedron), and a real-valued affine function

$$f(x_1, x_2, \ldots, x_n) = c_1 x_1 + c_2 x_2 + \cdots + c_n x_n + d$$

defined on this polytope, a _____ method will find a point in the polytope where this function has the smallest (or largest) value.

a. Slack variable
b. Linear programming
c. Linear programming relaxation
d. 1990 Clean Air Act

41. _____ is the study of how the variation (uncertainty) in the output of a mathematical model can be apportioned, qualitatively or quantitatively, to different sources of variation in the input of a model.

In more general terms uncertainty and sensitivity analyses investigate the robustness of a study when the study includes some form of mathematical modelling. While uncertainty analysis studies the overall uncertainty in the conclusions of the study, _____ tries to identify what source of uncertainty weights more on the study's conclusions.

a. Foreign ownership
c. No-bid contract
b. Policies and procedures
d. Sensitivity analysis

Chapter 6. Process Selection and Facility Layout

1. _____ is the process of determining the production capacity needed by an organization to meet changing demands for its products. In the context of _____, 'capacity' is the maximum amount of work that an organization is capable of completing in a given period of time.

A discrepancy between the capacity of an organization and the demands of its customers results in inefficiency, either in under-utilized resources or unfulfilled customers.

a. Capacity planning
b. Remanufacturing
c. Scientific management
d. Productivity

2. _____ is the use of control systems (such as numerical control, programmable logic control, and other industrial control systems), in concert with other applications of information technology (such as computer-aided technologies [CAD, CAM, CAx]), to control industrial machinery and processes, reducing the need for human intervention. In the scope of industrialization, _____ is a step beyond mechanization. Whereas mechanization provided human operators with machinery to assist them with the physical requirements of work, _____ greatly reduces the need for human sensory and mental requirements as well.

a. A4e
b. AAAI
c. A Stake in the Outcome
d. Automation

3. The phrase mergers and _____s refers to the aspect of corporate strategy, corporate finance and management dealing with the buying, selling and combining of different companies that can aid, finance, or help a growing company in a given industry grow rapidly without having to create another business entity.

An _____, also known as a takeover or a buyout, is the buying of one company (the 'target') by another. An _____ may be friendly or hostile.

a. A4e
b. AAAI
c. A Stake in the Outcome
d. Acquisition

4. _____ is, in very basic words, a position a firm occupies against its competitors.

According to Michael Porter, the three methods for creating a sustainable _____ are through:

1. Cost leadership

2. Differentiation

3. Focus (economics)

a. Competitive advantage
b. 1990 Clean Air Act
c. 28-hour day
d. Theory Z

5. _____ is an advertisement in which a particular product specifically mentions a competitor by name for the express purpose of showing why the competitor is inferior to the product naming it.

This should not be confused with parody advertisements, where a fictional product is being advertised for the purpose of poking fun at the particular advertisement, nor should it be confused with the use of a coined brand name for the purpose of comparing the product without actually naming an actual competitor. ('Wikipedia tastes better and is less filling than the Encyclopedia Galactica.')

In the 1980s, during what has been referred to as the cola wars, soft-drink manufacturer Pepsi ran a series of advertisements where people, caught on hidden camera, in a blind taste test, chose Pepsi over rival Coca-Cola.

a. Comparative advertising
b. 1990 Clean Air Act
c. 33 Strategies of War
d. 28-hour day

6. _____ is execution of a series of programs ('jobs') on a computer without human interaction.

Batch jobs are set up so they can be run to completion without human interaction, so all input data is preselected through scripts or command-line parameters. This is in contrast to 'online' or interactive programs which prompt the user for such input.

a. 33 Strategies of War
b. Batch processing
c. 1990 Clean Air Act
d. 28-hour day

7. _____ is an inventory strategy that strives to improve the return on investment of a business by reducing in-process inventory and its associated carrying costs. To meet _____ objectives, the process relies on signals between different points in the process. This means the process is often driven by a series of signals, or Kanban, which tell production when to make the next part. Kanban are usually 'tickets' but can be simple visual signals, such as the presence or absence of a part on a shelf. Implemented correctly, _____ can dramatically improve a manufacturing organization's return on investment, quality, and efficiency.

a. 33 Strategies of War
b. 28-hour day
c. 1990 Clean Air Act
d. Just-in-time

8. In probability theory, a probability distribution is called _____ if its cumulative distribution function is _____. This is equivalent to saying that for random variables X with the distribution in question, Pr[X = a] = 0 for all real numbers a, i.e.: the probability that X attains the value a is zero, for any number a. If the distribution of X is _____ then X is called a _____ random variable.

a. Connectionist expert systems
b. Pay Band
c. Decision tree pruning
d. Continuous

9. A _____ is a set of sequential operations established in a factory whereby materials are put through a refining process to produce an end-product that is suitable for onward consumption; or components are assembled to make a finished article.

Typically, raw materials such as metal ores or agricultural products such as foodstuffs or textile source plants (cotton, flax) require a sequence of treatments to render them useful. For metal, the processes include crushing, smelting and further refining.

Chapter 6. Process Selection and Facility Layout

a. Takt time
b. Theory of constraints
c. Six Sigma
d. Production line

10. An _____ is a manufacturing process in which parts (usually interchangeable parts) are added to a product in a sequential manner using optimally planned logistics to create a finished product much faster than with handcrafting-type methods. The _____ developed by Ford Motor Company between 1908 and 1915 made _____s famous in the following decade through the social ramifications of mass production, such as the affordability of the Ford Model T and the introduction of high wages for Ford workers. However, the various preconditions for the development at Ford stretched far back into the 19th century, from the gradual realization of the dream of interchangeability, to the concept of reinventing workflow and job descriptions using analytical methods.

a. A4e
b. Assembly line
c. A Stake in the Outcome
d. AAAI

11. _____ refers to the movement of cash into or out of a business or financial product. It is usually measured during a specified, finite period of time. Measurement of _____ can be used

- to determine a project's rate of return or value. The time of _____s into and out of projects are used as inputs in financial models such as internal rate of return, and net present value.
- to determine problems with a business's liquidity. Being profitable does not necessarily mean being liquid. A company can fail because of a shortage of cash, even while profitable.
- as an alternate measure of a business's profits when it is believed that accrual accounting concepts do not represent economic realities. For example, a company may be notionally profitable but generating little operational cash (as may be the case for a company that barters its products rather than selling for cash.) In such a case, the company may be deriving additional operating cash by issuing shares evaluating default risk, re-investment requirements, etc.

_____ is a generic term used differently depending on the context. It may be defined by users for their own purposes.

a. Gross profit margin
b. Cash flow
c. Gross profit
d. Sweat equity

12. _____ is the use of computer-based software tools that assist engineers and machinists in manufacturing or prototyping product components. Its primary purpose is to create a faster production process and components with more precise dimensions and material consistency, which in some cases, uses only the required amount of raw material (thus minimizing waste), while simultaneously reducing energy consumption. CAM is a programming tool that makes it possible to manufacture physical models using computer-aided design (CAD) programs.

a. Computer-aided manufacturing
b. 28-hour day
c. 33 Strategies of War
d. 1990 Clean Air Act

13. _____ is one of the managerial functions like planning, organizing, staffing and directing. It is an important function because it helps to check the errors and to take the corrective action so that deviation from standards are minimized and stated goals of the organization are achieved in desired manner. According to modern concepts, _____ is a foreseeing action whereas earlier concept of _____ was used only when errors were detected. _____ in management means setting standards, measuring actual performance and taking corrective action.

Chapter 6. Process Selection and Facility Layout

a. Decision tree pruning
c. Turnover
b. Schedule of reinforcement
d. Control

14. A _____ system is a manufacturing system in which there is some amount of flexibility that allows the system to react in the case of changes, whether predicted or unpredicted. This flexibility is generally considered to fall into two categories, which both contain numerous subcategories.

The first category, machine flexibility, covers the system's ability to be changed to produce new product types, and ability to change the order of operations executed on a part. The second category is called routing flexibility, which consists of the ability to use multiple machines to perform the same operation on a part, as well as the system's ability to absorb large-scale changes, such as in volume, capacity, or capability.

a. Flexible Manufacturing
c. Manufacturing resource planning
b. Jidoka
d. Homeworkers

15. _____ can be defined as the idea generation, concept development, testing and manufacturing or implementation of a physical object or service. _____ers conceptualize and evaluate ideas, making them tangible through products in a more systematic approach. The role of a _____er encompasses many characteristics of the marketing manager, product manager, industrial designer and design engineer.

a. Abraham Harold Maslow
c. Affiliation
b. Product design
d. Adam Smith

16. _____ has the following meanings:

The care and servicing by personnel for the purpose of maintaining equipment and facilities in satisfactory operating condition by providing for systematic inspection, detection, and correction of incipient failures either before they occur or before they develop into major defects.

1. Maintenance, including tests, measurements, adjustments, and parts replacement, performed specifically to prevent faults from occurring.

While _____ is generally considered to be worthwhile, there are risks such as equipment failure or human error involved when performing _____, just as in any maintenance operation. _____ as scheduled overhaul or scheduled replacement provides two of the three proactive failure management policies available to the maintenance engineer. Common methods of determining what _____ failure management policies should be applied are; OEM recommendations, requirements of codes and legislation within a jurisdiction, what an 'expert' thinks ought to be done, or the maintenance that's already done to similar equipment.

a. Preventive maintenance
c. 1990 Clean Air Act
b. 33 Strategies of War
d. 28-hour day

17. _____ is a model for workplace design, and is an integral part of lean manufacturing systems. The goal of lean manufacturing is the aggressive minimisation of waste, called muda, to achieve maximum efficiency of resources. _____, sometimes called cellular or cell production, arranges factory floor labor into semi-autonomous and multi-skilled teams, or work cells, who manufacture complete products or complex components.

Chapter 6. Process Selection and Facility Layout

a. Scientific management
c. Cellular Manufacturing
b. Productivity
d. Remanufacturing

18. In engineering and manufacturing, _____ and quality engineering are used in developing systems to ensure products or services are designed and produced to meet or exceed customer requirements. Refer to the definition by Merriam-Webster for further information . These systems are often developed in conjunction with other business and engineering disciplines using a cross-functional approach.
   a. Process capability
   c. Single Minute Exchange of Die
   b. Statistical process control
   d. Quality control

19. _____ is one of the many lean production methods for reducing waste in a manufacturing process. It provides a rapid and efficient way of converting a manufacturing process from running the current product to running the next product. This rapid changeover is key to reducing production lot sizes and thereby improving flow ' href='/wiki/Mura_'>Mura) The phrase 'single minute' does not mean that all changeovers and startups should take only one minute, but that they should take less than 10 minutes (in other words, 'single digit minute'.)
   a. Quality control
   c. Process capability
   b. Statistical process control
   d. Single Minute Exchange of Die

20. In quality assessment, _____ is an inspection standard describing the maximum number of defects that could be considered acceptable during the random sampling of an inspection. The defects found during inspection are classified into three levels: critical, major and minor. Broadly, these levels are defined as follows:

- Critical defects are those that render the product unsafe or hazardous for the end user, or that contravene mandatory regulations.

- Major defects can result in the product's failure, reducing its marketability, usability, or saleability.

- Minor defects do not affect the product's marketability or usability, but represent workmanship defects that make the product fall short of defined quality standards.

Different companies maintain different interpretations of each defect type.

   a. AAAI
   c. A Stake in the Outcome
   b. A4e
   d. Acceptable quality level

21. _____ in engineering is a method of manufacturing in which the entire production process is controlled by computer. The traditional separated process methods are joined through a computer by CIM. This integration allows that the processes exchange information with each other and they are able to initiate actions.
   a. 33 Strategies of War
   c. Computer-integrated manufacturing
   b. 1990 Clean Air Act
   d. 28-hour day

22. A _____ is a commercial building for storage of goods. _____s are used by manufacturers, importers, exporters, wholesalers, transport businesses, customs, etc. They are usually large plain buildings in industrial areas of cities and towns.

Chapter 6. Process Selection and Facility Layout

a. 1990 Clean Air Act
b. 33 Strategies of War
c. 28-hour day
d. Warehouse

23. _____ is an adjective for experience-based techniques that help in problem solving, learning and discovery. A _____ method is particularly used to rapidly come to a solution that is hoped to be close to the best possible answer, or 'optimal solution'. _____s are 'rules of thumb', educated guesses, intuitive judgments or simply common sense.

a. 1990 Clean Air Act
b. 28-hour day
c. Heuristic
d. Representativeness

24. The _____ Method is a tool for scheduling activities in a project plan. It is a method of constructing a project schedule network diagram that uses boxes, referred to as nodes, to represent activities and connects them with arrows that show the dependencies.

- Critical Tasks, noncritical tasks, and slack time
- Shows the relationship of the tasks to each other
- Allows for what-if, worst-case, best-case and most likely scenario

Key elements include determining predecessors and defining attributes such as

- early start date
- last-last
- early finish date
- late finish date
- Duration
- WBS reference

a. Project management office
b. Work package
c. Project manager
d. Precedence diagram

25. In economics, business, retail, and accounting, a _____ is the value of money that has been used up to produce something, and hence is not available for use anymore. In economics, a _____ is an alternative that is given up as a result of a decision. In business, the _____ may be one of acquisition, in which case the amount of money expended to acquire it is counted as _____.

a. Cost allocation
b. Cost
c. Cost overrun
d. Fixed costs

26. In mathematics, _____ is a technique for optimization of a linear objective function, subject to linear equality and linear inequality constraints. Informally, _____ determines the way to achieve the best outcome (such as maximum profit or lowest cost) in a given mathematical model and given some list of requirements represented as linear equations.

More formally, given a polytope (for example, a polygon or a polyhedron), and a real-valued affine function

$$f(x_1, x_2, \ldots, x_n) = c_1 x_1 + c_2 x_2 + \cdots + c_n x_n + d$$

defined on this polytope, a _____ method will find a point in the polytope where this function has the smallest (or largest) value.

a. 1990 Clean Air Act
b. Linear programming relaxation
c. Slack variable
d. Linear programming

27. In optimization (a branch of mathematics), a _____ is a member of a set of possible solutions to a given problem. A _____ does not have to be a likely or reasonable solution to the problem. The space of all _____s is called the feasible region, feasible set, search space, or solution space.

a. Gibbs state
b. 1990 Clean Air Act
c. Hann function
d. Candidate solution

28. The function f is called, variously, an _____, cost function, energy function, or energy functional. A feasible solution that minimizes (or maximizes, if that is the goal) the _____ is called an optimal solution.

Generally, when the feasible region or the _____ of the problem does not present convexity, there may be several local minima and maxima, where a local minimum x^* is defined as a point for which there exists some $>\delta > 0$ so that for all x such that

$$\boxed{x} >$$

the expression

$$\boxed{x} >$$

holds; that is to say, on some region around x^* all of the function values are greater than or equal to the value at that point.

a. AAAI
b. A4e
c. A Stake in the Outcome
d. Objective function

29. _____ of the learning curve effect and the closely related experience curve effect express the relationship between equations for experience and efficiency or between efficiency gains and investment in the effort. The experience of 'learning curves' was first observed by the 19th Century German psychologist Hermann Ebbinghaus according to the difficulty of memorizing varying numbers of verbal stimuli, and subsequent learning about the complex processes of learning are discussed in the

The rule used for representing the learning curve effect states that the more times a task has been performed, the less time will be required on each subsequent iteration.

Chapter 6. Process Selection and Facility Layout

a. Distribution
b. Spatial Decision Support Systems
c. Point biserial correlation coefficient
d. Models

30. 'Speaking generally, properties are those physical quantities which directly describe the physical attributes of the system; _____s are those combinations of the properties which suffice to determine the response of the system. Properties can have all sorts of dimensions, depending upon the system being considered; _____s are dimensionless, or have the dimension of time or its reciprocal.'

The term can also be used in engineering contexts, however, as it is typically used in the physical sciences.

When the terms formal _____ and actual _____ are used, they generally correspond with the definitions used in computer science.

a. Parameter
b. 33 Strategies of War
c. 1990 Clean Air Act
d. 28-hour day

31. _____ is a software based production planning and inventory control system used to manage manufacturing processes. Although it is not common nowadays, it is possible to conduct _____ by hand as well.

An _____ system is intended to simultaneously meet three objectives:

- Ensure materials and products are available for production and delivery to customers.
- Maintain the lowest possible level of inventory.
- Plan manufacturing activities, delivery schedules and purchasing activities.

Manufacturing organizations, whatever their products, face the same daily practical problem - that customers want products to be available in a shorter time than it takes to make them. This means that some level of planning is required.

a. Material requirements planning
b. 33 Strategies of War
c. 1990 Clean Air Act
d. 28-hour day

32. An unrelated, but similarly named method is the Nelder-Mead method or downhill _____ due to Nelder ' Mead (1965) and is a numerical method for optimizing many-dimensional unconstrained problems, belonging to the more general class of search algorithms.

In both cases, the method uses the concept of a simplex, which is a polytope of N + 1 vertices in N dimensions: a line segment in one dimension, a triangle in two dimensions, a tetrahedron in three-dimensional space and so forth.

A system of linear inequalities defines a polytope as a feasible region.

a. 33 Strategies of War
b. 28-hour day
c. Simplex method
d. 1990 Clean Air Act

Chapter 6. Process Selection and Facility Layout

33. _____ can be regarded as an outcome of mental processes (cognitive process) leading to the selection of a course of action among several alternatives. Every _____ process produces a final choice. The output can be an action or an opinion of choice.
   a. 1990 Clean Air Act
   b. 28-hour day
   c. 33 Strategies of War
   d. Decision making

34. _____ is the study of how the variation (uncertainty) in the output of a mathematical model can be apportioned, qualitatively or quantitatively, to different sources of variation in the input of a model.

In more general terms uncertainty and sensitivity analyses investigate the robustness of a study when the study includes some form of mathematical modelling. While uncertainty analysis studies the overall uncertainty in the conclusions of the study, _____ tries to identify what source of uncertainty weights more on the study's conclusions.

   a. Policies and procedures
   b. Foreign ownership
   c. No-bid contract
   d. Sensitivity analysis

35. _____ is one of the four Ps of the marketing mix. The other three aspects are product, promotion, and place. It is also a key variable in microeconomic price allocation theory.
   a. Penetration pricing
   b. Transfer pricing
   c. Price floor
   d. Pricing

Chapter 7. Design of Work Systems

1. _____s is the science of designing the job, equipment, and workplace to fit the worker. Proper _____ design is necessary to prevent repetitive strain injuries, which can develop over time and can lead to long-term disability.

_____s is concerned with the 'fit' between people and their work.

a. A Stake in the Outcome
b. A4e
c. AAAI
d. Ergonomic

2. In organizational development (OD), _____ is the application of Socio-Technical Systems principles and techniques to the humanization of work.

The aims of _____ to improved job satisfaction, to improved through-put, to improved quality and to reduced employee problems, e.g., grievances, absenteeism.

Under scientific management people would be directed by reason and the problems of industrial unrest would be appropriately (i.e., scientifically) addressed.

a. Path-goal theory
b. Graduate recruitment
c. Management process
d. Work design

3. _____ is subcontracting a process, such as product design or manufacturing, to a third-party company. The decision to outsource is often made in the interest of lowering cost or making better use of time and energy costs, redirecting or conserving energy directed at the competencies of a particular business, or to make more efficient use of land, labor, capital, (information) technology and resources. _____ became part of the business lexicon during the 1980s.

a. Opinion leadership
b. Outsourcing
c. Operant conditioning
d. Unemployment insurance

4. _____ is an inventory strategy that strives to improve the return on investment of a business by reducing in-process inventory and its associated carrying costs. To meet _____ objectives, the process relies on signals between different points in the process. This means the process is often driven by a series of signals, or Kanban, which tell production when to make the next part. Kanban are usually 'tickets' but can be simple visual signals, such as the presence or absence of a part on a shelf. Implemented correctly, _____ can dramatically improve a manufacturing organization's return on investment, quality, and efficiency.

a. 33 Strategies of War
b. Just-in-time
c. 28-hour day
d. 1990 Clean Air Act

5. _____ is a theory of management that analyzes and synthesizes workflows, with the objective of improving labour productivity. The core ideas of the theory were developed by Frederick Winslow Taylor in the 1880s and 1890s, and were first published in his monographs, Shop Management and The Principles of _____ Taylor believed that decisions based upon tradition and rules of thumb should be replaced by precise procedures developed after careful study of an individual at work.

a. Scientific management
b. Value engineering
c. Master production schedule
d. Capacity planning

6. _____, widely known as F. W. Taylor, was an American mechanical engineer who sought to improve industrial efficiency. He is regarded as the father of scientific management, and was one of the first management consultants.

Taylor was one of the intellectual leaders of the Efficiency Movement and his ideas, broadly conceived, were highly influential in the Progressive Era.

a. Jonah Jacob Goldberg
b. Frederick Winslow Taylor
c. Geoffrey Colvin
d. Douglas N. Daft

7. _____ means increasing the scope of a job through extending the range of its job duties and responsibilities. This contradicts the principles of specialisation and the division of labour whereby work is divided into small units, each of which is performed repetitively by an individual worker. Some motivational theories suggest that the boredom and alienation caused by the division of labour can actually cause efficiency to fall.

a. Job enlargement
b. Mock interview
c. Centralization
d. Delayering

8. _____ is an attempt to motivate employees by giving them the opportunity to use the range of their abilities. It is an idea that was developed by the American psychologist Frederick Herzberg in the 1950s. It can be contrasted to job enlargement which simply increases the number of tasks without changing the challenge.

a. Catfish effect
b. C-A-K-E
c. Cash cow
d. Job enrichment

9. _____ is an approach to management development where an individual is moved through a schedule of assignments designed to give him or her a breadth of exposure to the entire operation.

_____ is also practiced to allow qualified employees to gain more insights into the processes of a company, and to reduce boredom and increase job satisfaction through job variation.

The term _____ can also mean the scheduled exchange of persons in offices, especially in public offices, prior to the end of incumbency or the legislative period.

a. 33 Strategies of War
b. Job rotation
c. 28-hour day
d. 1990 Clean Air Act

10. _____ or lean production, which is often known simply as 'Lean', is a production practice that considers the expenditure of resources for any goal other than the creation of value for the end customer to be wasteful, and thus a target for elimination. Working from the perspective of the customer who consumes a product or service, 'value' is defined as any action or process that a customer would be willing to pay for. Basically, lean is centered around creating more value with less work.

a. Production line
b. Theory of constraints
c. Six Sigma
d. Lean manufacturing

11. _____ refers to various methodologies for analyzing the requirements of a job.

The general purpose of _____ is to document the requirements of a job and the work performed. Job and task analysis is performed as a basis for later improvements, including: definition of a job domain; describing a job; developing performance appraisals, selection systems, promotion criteria, training needs assessment, and compensation plans.

Chapter 7. Design of Work Systems

a. Work design
b. Hersey-Blanchard situational theory
c. Management process
d. Job analysis

12. Processes and activities include everything that happens within the _____. The term processes and activities is used instead of the term business process because many _____s do not contain highly structured business processes involving a prescribed sequence of steps, each of which is triggered in a pre-defined manner. Such processes are sometimes described as 'artful processes' whose sequence and content 'depend on the skills, experience, and judgment of the primary actors.' (Hill et al., 2006) In effect, business process is but one of a number of different perspectives for analyzing the activities within a _____.
   a. Split shift
   b. Work-at-home scheme
   c. Skilled worker
   d. Work system

13. _____ is a cross-disciplinary area concerned with protecting the safety, health and welfare of people engaged in work or employment. The goal of all _____ programs is to foster a work free safe environment. As a secondary effect, it may also protect co-workers, family members, employers, customers, suppliers, nearby communities, and other members of the public who are impacted by the workplace environment.
   a. Occupational Safety and Health
   b. AAAI
   c. A Stake in the Outcome
   d. A4e

14. The _____ is the primary federal law which governs occupational health and safety in the private sector and federal government in the United States. It was enacted by Congress in 1970 and was signed by President Richard Nixon on December 29, 1970. Its main goal is to ensure that employers provide employees with an environment free from recognized hazards, such as exposure to toxic chemicals, excessive noise levels, mechanical dangers, heat or cold stress, or unsanitary conditions.
   a. Unemployment and Farm Relief Act
   b. United States Department of Justice
   c. Occupational Safety and Health Act
   d. Unemployment Action Center

15. _____ can be regarded as an outcome of mental processes (cognitive process) leading to the selection of a course of action among several alternatives. Every _____ process produces a final choice. The output can be an action or an opinion of choice.
   a. 1990 Clean Air Act
   b. Decision making
   c. 33 Strategies of War
   d. 28-hour day

16. A time and motion study (or time-motion study) is a business efficiency technique combining the _____ work of Frederick Winslow Taylor with the Motion Study work of Frank and Lillian Gilbreth (not to be confused with their son, best known through the biographical 1950 film and book Cheaper by the Dozen.) It is a major part of scientific management (Taylorism.)

A time and motion study would be used to reduce the number of motions in performing a task in order to increase productivity.

   a. 1990 Clean Air Act
   b. 28-hour day
   c. 33 Strategies of War
   d. Time study

17. In economics and sociology, an _____ is any factor (financial or non-financial) that enables or motivates a particular course of action, or counts as a reason for preferring one choice to the alternatives. It is an expectation that encourages people to behave in a certain way. Since human beings are purposeful creatures, the study of _____ structures is central to the study of all economic activity (both in terms of individual decision-making and in terms of co-operation and competition within a larger institutional structure.)
    a. AAAI
    b. Incentive
    c. A Stake in the Outcome
    d. A4e

18. An _____ is a formal scheme used to promote or encourage specific actions or behavior by a specific group of people during a defined period of time. _____s are particularly used in business management to motivate employees, and in sales in order to attract and retain customers. The scientific literature also refers to this concept as Pay for Performance.
    a. A4e
    b. A Stake in the Outcome
    c. Incentive program
    d. AAAI

19. _____ describes types of employment in which a worker is paid a fixed 'piece rate' for each unit produced or action performed. _____ is also a form of performance-related pay (PRP) and is the oldest form of performance pay.

In a manufacturing setting, the output of piece work can be measured by the number of physical items (pieces) produced, such as when a garment worker is paid per operational step completed, regardless of the time required.

    a. Methods-time measurement
    b. Capacity planning
    c. Productivity
    d. Piecework

20. The term _____ refers to a graphical representation of the 'average' rate of learning for an activity or tool. It can represent at a glance the initial difficulty of learning something and, to an extent, how much there is to learn after initial familiarity. For example, the Windows program Notepad is extremely simple to learn, but offers little after this.
    a. 33 Strategies of War
    b. 1990 Clean Air Act
    c. Learning curve
    d. 28-hour day

Chapter 8. Location Planning and Analysis

1. In finance, an _____ is a contract between a buyer and a seller that gives the buyer the right--but not the obligation-- to buy or to sell a particular asset (the underlying asset) at a later day at an agreed price. In return for granting the _____, the seller collects a payment (the premium) from the buyer. A call _____ gives the buyer the right to buy the underlying asset; a put _____ gives the buyer of the _____ the right to sell the underlying asset.
   a. A Stake in the Outcome
   b. AAAI
   c. Option
   d. A4e

2. In economics, business, retail, and accounting, a _____ is the value of money that has been used up to produce something, and hence is not available for use anymore. In economics, a _____ is an alternative that is given up as a result of a decision. In business, the _____ may be one of acquisition, in which case the amount of money expended to acquire it is counted as _____.
   a. Fixed costs
   b. Cost allocation
   c. Cost overrun
   d. Cost

3. _____ is an inventory strategy that strives to improve the return on investment of a business by reducing in-process inventory and its associated carrying costs. To meet _____ objectives, the process relies on signals between different points in the process. This means the process is often driven by a series of signals, or Kanban, which tell production when to make the next part. Kanban are usually 'tickets' but can be simple visual signals, such as the presence or absence of a part on a shelf. Implemented correctly, _____ can dramatically improve a manufacturing organization's return on investment, quality, and efficiency.
   a. 33 Strategies of War
   b. 1990 Clean Air Act
   c. Just-in-time
   d. 28-hour day

4. _____ is an advertisement in which a particular product specifically mentions a competitor by name for the express purpose of showing why the competitor is inferior to the product naming it.

This should not be confused with parody advertisements, where a fictional product is being advertised for the purpose of poking fun at the particular advertisement, nor should it be confused with the use of a coined brand name for the purpose of comparing the product without actually naming an actual competitor. ('Wikipedia tastes better and is less filling than the Encyclopedia Galactica.')

In the 1980s, during what has been referred to as the cola wars, soft-drink manufacturer Pepsi ran a series of advertisements where people, caught on hidden camera, in a blind taste test, chose Pepsi over rival Coca-Cola.

   a. 28-hour day
   b. 1990 Clean Air Act
   c. Comparative advertising
   d. 33 Strategies of War

5. _____ is a type of trade policy that allows traders to act and transact without interference from government. Thus, the policy permits trading partners mutual gains from trade, with goods and services produced according to the theory of comparative advantage.

Under a _____ policy, prices are a reflection of true supply and demand, and are the sole determinant of resource allocation.

   a. 28-hour day
   b. 1990 Clean Air Act
   c. 33 Strategies of War
   d. Free Trade

Chapter 8. Location Planning and Analysis

6. _____ is a designated group of countries that have agreed to eliminate tariffs, quotas and preferences on most (if not all) goods and services traded between them. It can be considered the second stage of economic integration. Countries choose this kind of economic integration form if their economical structures are complementary.
   a. 1990 Clean Air Act
   b. Free trade area
   c. 33 Strategies of War
   d. 28-hour day

7. The _____ was the outcome of the failure of negotiating governments to create the International Trade Organization (ITO.) GATT was formed in 1947 and lasted until 1994, when it was replaced by the World Trade Organization. The Bretton Woods Conference had introduced the idea for an organization to regulate trade as part of a larger plan for economic recovery after World War II.
   a. 28-hour day
   b. 1990 Clean Air Act
   c. Multilateral treaty
   d. General Agreement on Tariffs and Trade

8. _____ in its literal sense is the process of transformation of local or regional phenomena into global ones. It can be described as a process by which the people of the world are unified into a single society and function together.

   This process is a combination of economic, technological, sociocultural and political forces.

   a. Histogram
   b. Cost Management
   c. Collaborative Planning, Forecasting and Replenishment
   d. Globalization

9. The _____ is a trilateral trade bloc in North America created by the governments of the United States, Canada, and Mexico. The agreement creating the trade bloc came into force on January 1, 1994. It superseded the Canada-United States Free Trade Agreement between the U.S. and Canada.
   a. North American Free Trade Agreement
   b. Business war game
   c. Career portfolios
   d. Trade union

10. In decision theory and estimation theory, the _____ of an estimator, $\hat{\theta}$, of an unknown parameter of the distribution, θ, is the expected value of the loss function

$$R(\theta, \hat{\theta}) = \mathbb{E}_\theta L(\theta, \hat{\theta}) = \int L(\theta, \hat{\theta}) \, dP_\theta.$$

Chapter 8. Location Planning and Analysis 63

where dP_θ is a probability measure parametrized by θ.

- For a scalar parameter θ and a quadratic loss function,

$$L(\theta, \hat{\theta}) = (\theta - \hat{\theta})^2$$

the _____ function becomes the mean squared error of the estimate,

$$R(\theta, \hat{\theta}) = E_\theta (\theta - \hat{\theta})^2$$

- In density estimation, the unknown parameter is probability density itself. The loss function is typically chosen to be a norm in an appropriate function space. For example, for L^2 norm,

$$L(f, \hat{f}) = \|f - \hat{f}\|_2^2$$

the _____ function becomes the mean integrated squared error

$$R(f, \hat{f}) = E\|f - \hat{f}\|^2$$

a. Risk
b. Financial modeling
c. Linear model
d. Risk aversion

11. _____ can be regarded as an outcome of mental processes (cognitive process) leading to the selection of a course of action among several alternatives. Every _____ process produces a final choice. The output can be an action or an opinion of choice.

a. 1990 Clean Air Act
b. Decision making
c. 33 Strategies of War
d. 28-hour day

12. In economics, _____ are business expenses that are not dependent on the activities of the business They tend to be time-related, such as salaries or rents being paid per month. This is in contrast to variable costs, which are volume-related (and are paid per quantity.)

In management accounting, _____ are defined as expenses that do not change in proportion to the activity of a business, within the relevant period or scale of production.

a. Cost of quality
b. Cost allocation
c. Transaction cost
d. Fixed costs

Chapter 8. Location Planning and Analysis

13. In economics, and cost accounting, _____ describes the total economic cost of production and is made up of variable costs, which vary according to the quantity of a good produced and include inputs such as labor and raw materials, plus fixed costs, which are independent of the quantity of a good produced and include inputs (capital) that cannot be varied in the short term, such as buildings and machinery. _____ in economics includes the total opportunity cost of each factor of production in addition to fixed and variable costs.

The rate at which _____ changes as the amount produced changes is called marginal cost.

a. Total cost
c. 28-hour day
b. 33 Strategies of War
d. 1990 Clean Air Act

14. _____ is a financial estimate designed to help consumers and enterprise managers assess direct and indirect costs It is a form of full cost accounting.

a. 1990 Clean Air Act
c. 33 Strategies of War
b. 28-hour day
d. Total cost of ownership

15. _____s are expenses that change in proportion to the activity of a business. In other words, _____ is the sum of marginal costs. It can also be considered normal costs.

a. Fixed costs
c. Variable cost
b. Cost accounting
d. Cost overrun

16. _____ is the state or fact of exclusive rights and control over property, which may be an object, land/real estate or intellectual property. An _____ right is also referred to as title. The concept of _____ has existed for thousands of years and in all cultures.

a. A Stake in the Outcome
c. A4e
b. Emanation of the state
d. Ownership

17. In mathematics, _____ is a technique for optimization of a linear objective function, subject to linear equality and linear inequality constraints. Informally, _____ determines the way to achieve the best outcome (such as maximum profit or lowest cost) in a given mathematical model and given some list of requirements represented as linear equations.

More formally, given a polytope (for example, a polygon or a polyhedron), and a real-valued affine function

$$f(x_1, x_2, \ldots, x_n) = c_1 x_1 + c_2 x_2 + \cdots + c_n x_n + d$$

defined on this polytope, a _____ method will find a point in the polytope where this function has the smallest (or largest) value.

a. 1990 Clean Air Act
c. Linear programming
b. Linear programming relaxation
d. Slack variable

Chapter 9. Management of Quality

1. In economics, business, retail, and accounting, a _____ is the value of money that has been used up to produce something, and hence is not available for use anymore. In economics, a _____ is an alternative that is given up as a result of a decision. In business, the _____ may be one of acquisition, in which case the amount of money expended to acquire it is counted as _____.
   a. Cost allocation
   b. Cost
   c. Cost overrun
   d. Fixed costs

2. _____ is one of the managerial functions like planning, organizing, staffing and directing. It is an important function because it helps to check the errors and to take the corrective action so that deviation from standards are minimized and stated goals of the organization are achieved in desired manner. According to modern concepts, _____ is a foreseeing action whereas earlier concept of _____ was used only when errors were detected. _____ in management means setting standards, measuring actual performance and taking corrective action.
   a. Control
   b. Turnover
   c. Schedule of reinforcement
   d. Decision tree pruning

3. _____ is a family of standards for quality management systems. _____ is maintained by ISO, the International Organization for Standardization and is administered by accreditation and certification bodies. The rules are updated, the time and changes in the requirements for quality, motivate change.
   a. AAAI
   b. A Stake in the Outcome
   c. ISO 9000
   d. A4e

4. The _____ was a period in the late 18th and early 19th centuries when major changes in agriculture, manufacturing, mining, and transportation had a profound effect on the socioeconomic and cultural conditions in Britain. The changes subsequently spread throughout Europe, North America, and eventually the world. The onset of the _____ marked a major turning point in human society; almost every aspect of daily life was eventually influenced in some way.
   a. Industrial Revolution
   b. Affiliation
   c. Abraham Harold Maslow
   d. Adam Smith

5. In engineering and manufacturing, _____ and quality engineering are used in developing systems to ensure products or services are designed and produced to meet or exceed customer requirements. Refer to the definition by Merriam-Webster for further information. These systems are often developed in conjunction with other business and engineering disciplines using a cross-functional approach.
   a. Statistical process control
   b. Process capability
   c. Single Minute Exchange of Die
   d. Quality Control

6. _____ is a theory of management that analyzes and synthesizes workflows, with the objective of improving labour productivity. The core ideas of the theory were developed by Frederick Winslow Taylor in the 1880s and 1890s, and were first published in his monographs, Shop Management and The Principles of _____ Taylor believed that decisions based upon tradition and rules of thumb should be replaced by precise procedures developed after careful study of an individual at work.
   a. Scientific management
   b. Value engineering
   c. Capacity planning
   d. Master production schedule

7. _____, widely known as F. W. Taylor, was an American mechanical engineer who sought to improve industrial efficiency. He is regarded as the father of scientific management, and was one of the first management consultants.

Taylor was one of the intellectual leaders of the Efficiency Movement and his ideas, broadly conceived, were highly influential in the Progressive Era.

a. Douglas N. Daft
b. Geoffrey Colvin
c. Frederick Winslow Taylor
d. Jonah Jacob Goldberg

8. '_____' is Step 7 of 'Philip Crosby's 14 Step Quality Improvement Process' . Although applicable to any type of enterprise, it has been primarily adopted within industry supply chains wherever large volumes of components are being purchased (common items such as nuts and bolts are good examples.)

_____ was a quality control program originated by the Denver Division of the Martin Marietta Corporation (now Lockheed Martin) on the Titan Missile program, which carried the first astronauts into space in the late 1960s.

a. Zero defects
b. 28-hour day
c. Root cause analysis
d. 1990 Clean Air Act

9. _____ is an effective method of monitoring a process through the use of control charts. Control charts enable the use of objective criteria for distinguishing background variation from events of significance based on statistical techniques. Much of its power lies in the ability to monitor both process center and its variation about that center.

a. Process capability
b. Quality control
c. Single Minute Exchange of Die
d. Statistical process control

10. _____ is a Japanese philosophy that focuses on continuous improvement throughout all aspects of life. When applied to the workplace, _____ activities continually improve all functions of a business, from manufacturing to management and from the CEO to the assembly line workers. By improving standardized activities and processes, _____ aims to eliminate waste .

a. Kaizen
b. Sensitivity analysis
c. Cross-docking
d. Psychological pricing

11. A _____ is a volunteer group composed of workers (or even students), usually under the leadership of their supervisor (but they can elect a team leader), who are trained to identify, analyse and solve work-related problems and present their solutions to management in order to improve the performance of the organization, and motivate and enrich the work of employees. When matured, true _____s become self-managing, having gained the confidence of management.
_____s are an alternative to the dehumanising concept of the Division of Labour, where workers or individuals are treated like robots.

a. Connectionist expert systems
b. Certified in Production and Inventory Management
c. Quality circle
d. Competency-based job descriptions

12. The _____ is a graphical depiction of loss developed by the Japanese business statistician Genichi Taguchi to describe a phenomenon affecting the value of products produced by a company. Praised by Dr. W. Edwards Deming, it made clear the concept that quality does not suddenly plummet when, for instance, a machinist exceeds a rigid blueprint tolerance. Instead 'loss' in value progressively increases as variation increases from the intended condition. This was considered a breakthrough in describing quality, and helped fuel the continuous improvement movement that since has become known as lean manufacturing.

Chapter 9. Management of Quality

a. 1990 Clean Air Act
b. 28-hour day
c. 33 Strategies of War
d. Taguchi loss function

13. In statistics, decision theory and economics, a _____ is a function that maps an event (technically an element of a sample space) onto a real number representing the economic cost or regret associated with the event.

Less technically, in statistics a _____ represents the loss (cost in money or loss in utility in some other sense) associated with an estimate being 'wrong' (different from either a desired or a true value) as a function of a measure of the degree of wrongness (generally the difference between the estimated value and the true or desired value.)

Both Frequentist and Bayesian statistical theory involve calculating statistics in such a way as to minimize the expected loss observed from being wrong given a set of assumptions about the data and one's _____.

a. 33 Strategies of War
b. Loss function
c. 1990 Clean Air Act
d. 28-hour day

14. _____ is an advertisement in which a particular product specifically mentions a competitor by name for the express purpose of showing why the competitor is inferior to the product naming it.

This should not be confused with parody advertisements, where a fictional product is being advertised for the purpose of poking fun at the particular advertisement, nor should it be confused with the use of a coined brand name for the purpose of comparing the product without actually naming an actual competitor. ('Wikipedia tastes better and is less filling than the Encyclopedia Galactica.')

In the 1980s, during what has been referred to as the cola wars, soft-drink manufacturer Pepsi ran a series of advertisements where people, caught on hidden camera, in a blind taste test, chose Pepsi over rival Coca-Cola.

a. 1990 Clean Air Act
b. 33 Strategies of War
c. 28-hour day
d. Comparative advertising

15. _____ is the area of law in which manufacturers, distributors, suppliers, retailers, and others who make products available to the public are held responsible for the injuries those products cause.

In the United States, the claims most commonly associated with _____ are negligence, strict liability, breach of warranty, and various consumer protection claims. The majority of _____ laws are determined at the state level and vary widely from state to state.

a. Railway Labor Act
b. Leave of absence
c. Right-to-work laws
d. Product liability

16. Quality management can be considered to have three main components: quality control, quality assurance and _____. Quality management is focused not only on product quality, but also the means to achieve it. Quality management therefore uses quality assurance and control of processes as well as products to achieve more consistent quality.

a. 1990 Clean Air Act
b. 28-hour day
c. Quality management
d. Quality Improvement

17. _____ can be regarded as an outcome of mental processes (cognitive process) leading to the selection of a course of action among several alternatives. Every _____ process produces a final choice. The output can be an action or an opinion of choice.
   a. 28-hour day
   b. 33 Strategies of War
   c. Decision making
   d. 1990 Clean Air Act

18. The _____, widely known as ISO , is an international-standard-setting body composed of representatives from various national standards organizations. Founded on 23 February 1947, the organization promulgates worldwide proprietary industrial and commercial standards. It is headquartered in Geneva, Switzerland.
   a. A Stake in the Outcome
   b. A4e
   c. International Organization for Standardization
   d. AAAI

19. In probability theory, a probability distribution is called _____ if its cumulative distribution function is _____. This is equivalent to saying that for random variables X with the distribution in question, Pr[X = a] = 0 for all real numbers a, i.e.: the probability that X attains the value a is zero, for any number a. If the distribution of X is _____ then X is called a _____ random variable.
   a. Connectionist expert systems
   b. Pay Band
   c. Decision tree pruning
   d. Continuous

20. _____ is a management process whereby delivery (customer valued) processes are constantly evaluated and improved in the light of their efficiency, effectiveness and flexibility.

Some see it as a meta process for most management systems (Business Process Management, Quality Management, Project Management). Deming saw it as part of the 'system' whereby feedback from the process and customer were evaluated against organisational goals.

   a. Sole proprietorship
   b. Continuous Improvement Process
   c. First-mover advantage
   d. Critical Success Factor

21. _____, a business term, is a measure of how products and services supplied by a company meet or surpass customer expectation. It is seen as a key performance indicator within business and is part of the four perspectives of a Balanced Scorecard.

In a competitive marketplace where businesses compete for customers, _____ is seen as a key differentiator and increasingly has become a key element of business strategy.

   a. Horizontal integration
   b. Critical Success Factor
   c. Foreign ownership
   d. Customer satisfaction

22. _____ is a Japanese term that means 'fail-safing' or 'mistake-proofing'. A _____ is any mechanism in a Lean manufacturing process that helps an equipment operator avoid (yokeru) mistakes (poka.) Its purpose is to eliminate product defects by preventing, correcting, or drawing attention to human errors as they occur.

a. 1990 Clean Air Act
c. 28-hour day
b. 33 Strategies of War
d. Poka-yoke

23. _____ is a business management strategy aimed at embedding awareness of quality in all organizational processes. _____ has been widely used in manufacturing, education, hospitals, call centers, government, and service industries, as well as NASA space and science programs.

As defined by the International Organization for Standardization (ISO):

> '_____ is a management approach for an organization, centered on quality, based on the participation of all its members and aiming at long-term success through customer satisfaction, and benefits to all members of the organization and to society.' ISO 8402:1994

One major aim is to reduce variation from every process so that greater consistency of effort is obtained. (Royse, D., Thyer, B., Padgett D., ' Logan T., 2006)

a. Total quality management
c. 1990 Clean Air Act
b. 28-hour day
d. Quality management

24. _____ can be considered to have three main components: quality control, quality assurance and quality improvement. _____ is focused not only on product quality, but also the means to achieve it. _____ therefore uses quality assurance and control of processes as well as products to achieve more consistent quality.

a. 28-hour day
c. 1990 Clean Air Act
b. Quality management
d. Total quality management

25. _____ is the process of comparing the cost, cycle time, productivity, or quality of a specific process or method to another that is widely considered to be an industry standard or best practice. Essentially, _____ provides a snapshot of the performance of your business and helps you understand where you are in relation to a particular standard. The result is often a business case for making changes in order to make improvements.

a. Cost leadership
c. Benchmarking
b. Competitive heterogeneity
d. Complementors

26. _____ refers to increasing the spiritual, political, social or economic strength of individuals and communities. It often involves the empowered developing confidence in their own capacities.

The term Human _____ covers a vast landscape of meanings, interpretations, definitions and disciplines ranging from psychology and philosophy to the highly commercialized Self-Help industry and Motivational sciences.

a. A4e
c. A Stake in the Outcome
b. AAAI
d. Empowerment

27. _____ is a business management strategy, initially implemented by Motorola, that today enjoys widespread application in many sectors of industry.

Chapter 9. Management of Quality

_____ seeks to improve the quality of process outputs by identifying and removing the causes of defects (errors) and variation in manufacturing and business processes. It uses a set of quality management methods, including statistical methods, and creates a special infrastructure of people within the organization ('Black Belts' etc.)

- a. Production line
- b. Takt time
- c. Theory of constraints
- d. Six sigma

28. _____ ('Plan-Do-Check-Act') is an iterative four-step problem-solving process typically used in business process improvement. It is also known as the Deming Cycle, Shewhart cycle, Deming Wheel, or Plan-Do-Study-Act.

_____ was made popular by Dr. W. Edwards Deming, who is considered by many to be the father of modern quality control; however it was always referred to by him as the Shewhart cycle. Later in Deming's career, he modified _____ to Plan, Do, Study, Act (PDSA) so as to better describe his recommendations.

- a. Management team
- b. Management by exception
- c. PDCA
- d. Decentralization

29. In organizational development (OD), _____ is a series of actions taken by a Process Owner to identify, analyze and improve existing processes within an organization to meet new goals and objectives. These actions often follow a specific methodology or strategy to create successful results. A sampling of these are listed below.
- a. Product innovation
- b. Letter of resignation
- c. Supervisory board
- d. Process improvement

30. A _____ is a common type of chart, that represents an algorithm or process, showing the steps as boxes of various kinds, and their order by connecting these with arrows. _____s are used in analyzing, designing, documenting or managing a process or program in various fields.

The first structured method for documenting process flow, the 'flow process chart', was introduced by Frank Gilbreth to members of ASME in 1921 as the presentation 'Process Charts--First Steps in Finding the One Best Way'.

- a. 33 Strategies of War
- b. 1990 Clean Air Act
- c. Flowchart
- d. 28-hour day

31. The _____ in statistical process control is a tool used to determine whether a manufacturing or business process is in a state of statistical control or not.

If the chart indicates that the process is currently under control then it can be used with confidence to predict the future performance of the process. If the chart indicates that the process being monitored is not in control, the pattern it reveals can help determine the source of variation to be eliminated to bring the process back into control.

a. Simple moving average
b. Control chart
c. Time series analysis
d. Failure rate

32. In statistics, a _____ is a graphical display of tabulated frequencies, shown as bars. It shows what proportion of cases fall into each of several categories: it is a form of data binning. The categories are usually specified as non-overlapping intervals of some variable.
   a. Standard deviation
   b. Correlation
   c. Statistics
   d. Histogram

33. A scatter plot is a type of display using Cartesian coordinates to display values for two variables for a set of data.

The data is displayed as a collection of points, each having the value of one variable determining the position on the horizontal axis and the value of the other variable determining the position on the vertical axis. A scatter plot is also called a scatter chart, _____ and scatter graph.

   a. 1990 Clean Air Act
   b. 33 Strategies of War
   c. 28-hour day
   d. Scatter diagram

34. _____ is a statistical technique in decision making that is used for selection of a limited number of tasks that produce significant overall effect. It uses the Pareto principle - the idea that by doing 20% of work you can generate 80% of the advantage of doing the entire job. Or in terms of quality improvement, a large majority of problems (80%) are produced by a few key causes (20%.)
   a. Probability matching
   b. Goodness of fit
   c. Polychoric correlation
   d. Pareto analysis

35. _____s are diagrams that show the causes of a certain event. A common use of the _____ is in product design, to identify potential factors causing an overall effect.

_____s were proposed by Kaoru Ishikawa in the 1960s, who pioneered quality management processes in the Kawasaki shipyards, and in the process became one of the founding fathers of modern management.

   a. AAAI
   b. A4e
   c. A Stake in the Outcome
   d. Ishikawa diagram

36. A _____, also known as a run-sequence plot is a graph that displays observed data in a time sequence. Often, the data displayed represent some aspect of the output or performance of a manufacturing or other business process.

Run sequence plots are an easy way to graphically summarize a univariate data set.

   a. 28-hour day
   b. Run chart
   c. 1990 Clean Air Act
   d. 33 Strategies of War

37. _____ is a group creativity technique designed to generate a large number of ideas for the solution of a problem. The method was first popularized in the late 1930s by Alex Faickney Osborn in a book called Applied Imagination. Osborn proposed that groups could double their creative output with _____.

a. Adam Smith
b. Affiliation
c. Abraham Harold Maslow
d. Brainstorming

38. The _____ is a business tool used to organize ideas and data. It is one of the Seven Management and Planning Tools.

The tool is commonly used within project management and allows large numbers of ideas to be sorted into groups for review and analysis.

The _____ was devised by Jiro Kawakita in the 1960s and is sometimes referred to as the KJ Method.

a. AAAI
b. A Stake in the Outcome
c. A4e
d. Affinity diagram

39. In financial accounting, a _____ or statement of financial position is a summary of a person's or organization's balances. Assets, liabilities and ownership equity are listed as of a specific date, such as the end of its financial year. A _____ is often described as a snapshot of a company's financial condition.

a. Balance sheet
b. 28-hour day
c. 1990 Clean Air Act
d. 33 Strategies of War

Chapter 10. Quality Control

1. In engineering and manufacturing, _____ and quality engineering are used in developing systems to ensure products or services are designed and produced to meet or exceed customer requirements. Refer to the definition by Merriam-Webster for further information. These systems are often developed in conjunction with other business and engineering disciplines using a cross-functional approach.
   - a. Process capability
   - b. Single Minute Exchange of Die
   - c. Statistical process control
   - d. Quality control

2. _____ is one of the managerial functions like planning, organizing, staffing and directing. It is an important function because it helps to check the errors and to take the corrective action so that deviation from standards are minimized and stated goals of the organization are achieved in desired manner. According to modern concepts, _____ is a foreseeing action whereas earlier concept of _____ was used only when errors were detected. _____ in management means setting standards, measuring actual performance and taking corrective action.
   - a. Decision tree pruning
   - b. Control
   - c. Schedule of reinforcement
   - d. Turnover

3. In quality assessment, _____ is an inspection standard describing the maximum number of defects that could be considered acceptable during the random sampling of an inspection. The defects found during inspection are classified into three levels: critical, major and minor. Broadly, these levels are defined as follows:

   - Critical defects are those that render the product unsafe or hazardous for the end user, or that contravene mandatory regulations.
   - Major defects can result in the product's failure, reducing its marketability, usability, or saleability.
   - Minor defects do not affect the product's marketability or usability, but represent workmanship defects that make the product fall short of defined quality standards.

   Different companies maintain different interpretations of each defect type.
   - a. Acceptable quality level
   - b. A4e
   - c. A Stake in the Outcome
   - d. AAAI

4. The _____ in statistical process control is a tool used to determine whether a manufacturing or business process is in a state of statistical control or not.

   If the chart indicates that the process is currently under control then it can be used with confidence to predict the future performance of the process. If the chart indicates that the process being monitored is not in control, the pattern it reveals can help determine the source of variation to be eliminated to bring the process back into control.
   - a. Simple moving average
   - b. Control chart
   - c. Failure rate
   - d. Time series analysis

5. _____ is an effective method of monitoring a process through the use of control charts. Control charts enable the use of objective criteria for distinguishing background variation from events of significance based on statistical techniques. Much of its power lies in the ability to monitor both process center and its variation about that center.

a. Statistical process control
c. Quality control
b. Single Minute Exchange of Die
d. Process capability

6. _____ are horizontal lines drawn on an statistical process control chart, usually at a distance of >±3 standard deviations of the plotted statistic from the statistic's mean.

For normally distributed statistics, the area bracketed by the _____ will on average contain 99.73% of all the plot points on the chart, as long as the process is and remains in statistical control.

_____ should not be confused with tolerance limits, which are completely independent of the distribution of the plotted sample statistic.

a. Skewness risk
c. T-statistic
b. Control limits
d. 1990 Clean Air Act

7. _____ is one of the four elements of marketing mix. An organization or set of organizations (go-betweens) involved in the process of making a product or service available for use or consumption by a consumer or business user.

The other three parts of the marketing mix are product, pricing, and promotion.

a. Distribution
c. Job creation programs
b. Missing completely at random
d. Matching theory

8. In probability theory, the _____ states conditions under which the sum of a sufficiently large number of independent random variables, each with finite mean and variance, will be approximately normally distributed. Since real-world quantities are often the balanced sum of many unobserved random events, this theorem provides a partial explanation for the prevalence of the normal probability distribution. The _____ also justifies the approximation of large-sample statistics to the normal distribution in controlled experiments.

a. Point biserial correlation coefficient
c. Heavy-tailed distributions
b. Pay Band
d. Central limit theorem

9. In decision theory and estimation theory, the _____ of an estimator, $\hat{\theta}$, of an unknown parameter of the distribution, θ, is the expected value of the loss function

$$R(\theta, \hat{\theta}) = \mathbb{E}_\theta L(\theta, \hat{\theta}) = \int L(\theta, \hat{\theta}) \, dP_\theta.$$

Chapter 10. Quality Control 75

where dP_θ is a probability measure parametrized by θ.

- For a scalar parameter θ and a quadratic loss function,

$$L(\theta, \hat{\theta}) = (\theta - \hat{\theta})^2$$

the _____ function becomes the mean squared error of the estimate,

$$R(\theta, \hat{\theta}) = E_\theta (\theta - \hat{\theta})^2$$

- In density estimation, the unknown parameter is probability density itself. The loss function is typically chosen to be a norm in an appropriate function space. For example, for L^2 norm,

$$L(f, \hat{f}) = \|f - \hat{f}\|_2^2$$

the _____ function becomes the mean integrated squared error

$$R(f, \hat{f}) = E\|f - \hat{f}\|^2$$

a. Risk
c. Risk aversion
b. Financial modeling
d. Linear model

10. In statistics, _____ is:

- the arithmetic _____
- the expected value of a random variable, which is also called the population _____.

It is sometimes stated that the '_____' _____s average. This is incorrect if '_____' is taken in the specific sense of 'arithmetic _____' as there are different types of averages: the _____, median, and mode. Other simple statistical analyses use measures of spread, such as range, interquartile range, or standard deviation. For a real-valued random variable X, the _____ is the expectation of X. Note that not every probability distribution has a defined _____; see the Cauchy distribution for an example.

a. Correlation
c. Mean
b. Statistical inference
d. Control chart

11. An _____ is a specific member of a family of control charts. A control chart is a tool used in quality control, specifically SPC or statistical process control, as originally developed by Walter A. Shewhart at Western Electric in 1924 to improve the quality of telephones.

A control chart is a plot of measurements of a product on two special scales, usually located above and below each other and running horizontally. _____s consist of two charts, both with the same horizontal axis denoting the sample number.

a. X-bar/R chart
b. 1990 Clean Air Act
c. 28-hour day
d. 33 Strategies of War

12. The term '_____' refers to the concept of collecting information and attempting to spot a pattern in the information. In some fields of study, the term '_____' has more formally-defined meanings.

In project management _____ is a mathematical technique that uses historical results to predict future outcome.

a. Regression analysis
b. Least squares
c. Stepwise regression
d. Trend analysis

13. _____ is a Japanese philosophy that focuses on continuous improvement throughout all aspects of life. When applied to the workplace, _____ activities continually improve all functions of a business, from manufacturing to management and from the CEO to the assembly line workers. By improving standardized activities and processes, _____ aims to eliminate waste.

a. Sensitivity analysis
b. Psychological pricing
c. Kaizen
d. Cross-docking

14. The _____ is a measurable property of a process to the specification, expressed as a _____ index (e.g., C_{pk} or C_{pm}) or as a process performance index (e.g., P_{pk} or P_{pm}.) The output of this measurement is usually illustrated by a histogram and calculations that predict how many parts will be produced out of specification.

_____ is also defined as the capability of a process to meet its purpose as managed by an organization's management and process definition structures ISO 15504.

a. Process capability
b. Statistical process control
c. Quality control
d. Single Minute Exchange of Die

15. Engineering _____ is the permissible limit of variation in

1. a physical dimension,
2. a measured value or physical property of a material, manufactured object, system, or service,
3. other measured values (such as temperature, humidity, etc.)
4. in engineering and safety, a physical distance or space (_____), as in a truck (lorry), train or boat under a bridge as well as a train in a tunnel

Dimensions, properties, or conditions may vary within certain practical limits without significantly affecting functioning of equipment or a process. _____s are specified to allow reasonable leeway for imperfections and inherent variability without compromising performance.

The _____ may be specified as a factor or percentage of the nominal value, a maximum deviation from a nominal value, an explicit range of allowed values, be specified by a note or published standard with this information, or be implied by the numeric accuracy of the nominal value. _____ can be symmetrical, as in 40±0.1, or asymmetrical, such as 40+0.2/−0.1.

a. Quality assurance
c. Zero defects
b. Root cause analysis
d. Tolerance

16. _____ is a business management strategy, initially implemented by Motorola, that today enjoys widespread application in many sectors of industry.

_____ seeks to improve the quality of process outputs by identifying and removing the causes of defects (errors) and variation in manufacturing and business processes. It uses a set of quality management methods, including statistical methods, and creates a special infrastructure of people within the organization ('Black Belts' etc.)

a. Theory of constraints
c. Production line
b. Six sigma
d. Takt time

17. A barcode (also bar code) is an optical machine-readable representation of data. Originally, _____ represented data in the widths (lines) and the spacings of parallel lines, and may be referred to as linear or 1D (1 dimensional) barcodes or symbologies. They also come in patterns of squares, dots, hexagons and other geometric patterns within images termed 2D (2 dimensional) matrix codes or symbologies.

a. 28-hour day
c. 1990 Clean Air Act
b. Bar Codes
d. 33 Strategies of War

18. _____ is the process of comparing the cost, cycle time, productivity, or quality of a specific process or method to another that is widely considered to be an industry standard or best practice. Essentially, _____ provides a snapshot of the performance of your business and helps you understand where you are in relation to a particular standard. The result is often a business case for making changes in order to make improvements.

a. Complementors
c. Cost leadership
b. Competitive heterogeneity
d. Benchmarking

Chapter 11. Supply Chain Management

1. A _____ is the system of organizations, people, technology, activities, information and resources involved in moving a product or service from supplier to customer. _____ activities transform natural resources, raw materials and components into a finished product that is delivered to the end customer. In sophisticated _____ systems, used products may re-enter the _____ at any point where residual value is recyclable.
   - a. Wholesalers
   - b. Packaging
   - c. Drop shipping
   - d. Supply chain

2. _____ is the management of a network of interconnected businesses involved in the ultimate provision of product and service packages required by end customers (Harland, 1996.) _____ spans all movement and storage of raw materials, work-in-process inventory, and finished goods from point of origin to point of consumption (supply chain.)

   The definition an American professional association put forward is that _____ encompasses the planning and management of all activities involved in sourcing, procurement, conversion, and logistics management activities.

   - a. Freight forwarder
   - b. Packaging
   - c. Drop shipping
   - d. Supply chain management

3. _____ is the process of determining the production capacity needed by an organization to meet changing demands for its products. In the context of _____, 'capacity' is the maximum amount of work that an organization is capable of completing in a given period of time.

   A discrepancy between the capacity of an organization and the demands of its customers results in inefficiency, either in under-utilized resources or unfulfilled customers.

   - a. Scientific management
   - b. Remanufacturing
   - c. Productivity
   - d. Capacity planning

4. _____ is a concept that aims to enhance supply chain integration by supporting and assisting joint practices. _____ seeks cooperative management of inventory through joint visibility and replenishment of products throughout the supply chain. Information shared between suppliers and retailers aids in planning and satisfying customer demands through a supportive system of shared information.
   - a. Collaborative Planning, Forecasting and Replenishment
   - b. Career portfolios
   - c. Timesheets
   - d. Groups decision making

5. In economics, _____ is the desire to own something and the ability to pay for it. The term _____ signifies the ability or the willingness to buy a particular commodity at a given point of time.
   - a. 1990 Clean Air Act
   - b. 33 Strategies of War
   - c. 28-hour day
   - d. Demand

Chapter 11. Supply Chain Management

6. A _____ is composed of the enterprises that sell the goods or services.

- Distributors
- Resellers
- Catalog sellers
- Site rentiers
- Wholesellers

Some clubs have socnet style webpages for arranging club outings and travel for small groups of 5 - 16 people. This is motivated by the customers and is an asset for the clubs.

Some customers are uniting to purchase goods from a specific supplier.

a. Supply Chain Risk Management
c. Delayed differentiation
b. Supply-Chain Operations Reference
d. Demand chain

7. _____ is the management of the flow of goods, information and other resources, including energy and people, between the point of origin and the point of consumption in order to meet the requirements of consumers (frequently, and originally, military organizations.) _____ involves the integration of information, transportation, inventory, warehousing, material-handling, and packaging, and occasionally security. _____ is a channel of the supply chain which adds the value of time and place utility.

a. 1990 Clean Air Act
c. 28-hour day
b. Third-party logistics
d. Logistics

8. The _____ is a concept from business management that was first described and popularized by Michael Porter in his 1985 best-seller, Competitive Advantage: Creating and Sustaining Superior Performance.

A _____ is a chain of activities. Products pass through all activities of the chain in order and at each activity the product gains some value. The chain of activities gives the products more added value than the sum of added values of all activities. It is important not to mix the concept of the _____ with the costs occurring throughout the activities.

a. Market development
c. Mass marketing
b. Customer relationship management
d. Value chain

9. In economics, business, retail, and accounting, a _____ is the value of money that has been used up to produce something, and hence is not available for use anymore. In economics, a _____ is an alternative that is given up as a result of a decision. In business, the _____ may be one of acquisition, in which case the amount of money expended to acquire it is counted as _____.

a. Fixed costs
c. Cost allocation
b. Cost
d. Cost overrun

10. _____, commonly referred to as 'eBusiness' or 'e-Business', may be defined as the utilization of information and communication technologies (ICT) in support of all the activities of business. Commerce constitutes the exchange of products and services between businesses, groups and individuals and hence can be seen as one of the essential activities of any business. Hence, electronic commerce or eCommerce focuses on the use of ICT to enable the external activities and relationships of the business with individuals, groups and other businesses .

a. A Stake in the Outcome
b. AAAI
c. A4e
d. Electronic business

11. _____ is subcontracting a process, such as product design or manufacturing, to a third-party company. The decision to outsource is often made in the interest of lowering cost or making better use of time and energy costs, redirecting or conserving energy directed at the competencies of a particular business, or to make more efficient use of land, labor, capital, (information) technology and resources. _____ became part of the business lexicon during the 1980s.

a. Opinion leadership
b. Outsourcing
c. Operant conditioning
d. Unemployment insurance

12. The _____ is an observed phenomenon in forecast-driven distribution channels. The concept has its roots in J Forrester's Industrial Dynamics (1961) and thus it is also known as the Forrester Effect. Since the oscillating demand magnification upstream a supply chain reminds someone of a cracking whip it became famous as the _____.

a. 28-hour day
b. Bullwhip effect
c. 1990 Clean Air Act
d. 33 Strategies of War

13. _____ is a family of business models in which the buyer of a product provides certain information to a supplier of that product and the supplier takes full responsibility for maintaining an agreed inventory of the material, usually at the buyer's consumption location (usually a store.) A third party logistics provider can also be involved to make sure that the buyer has the required level of inventory by adjusting the demand and supply gaps.

As a symbiotic relationship, _____ makes it less likely that a business will unintentionally become out of stock of a good and reduces inventory in the supply chain.

a. Supply Chain Risk Management
b. Delayed differentiation
c. Supply-Chain Operations Reference
d. Vendor Managed Inventory

14. _____ is a business function that provides a response to customer order enquiries, based on resource availability. It generates available quantities of the requested product, and delivery due dates. Therefore, _____ supports order promising and fulfillment, aiming to manage demand and match it to production plans.

a. AAAI
b. Available-to-promise
c. A Stake in the Outcome
d. A4e

15. In decision theory and estimation theory, the _____ of an estimator, $\hat{\theta}$, of an unknown parameter of the distribution, θ, is the expected value of the loss function

$$R(\theta, \hat{\theta}) = \mathbb{E}_\theta L(\theta, \hat{\theta}) = \int L(\theta, \hat{\theta}) \, dP_\theta.$$

Chapter 11. Supply Chain Management

where dP_θ is a probability measure parametrized by θ.

- For a scalar parameter θ and a quadratic loss function,

$$L(\theta, \hat{\theta}) = (\theta - \hat{\theta})^2$$

the _____ function becomes the mean squared error of the estimate,

$$R(\theta, \hat{\theta}) = E_\theta (\theta - \hat{\theta})^2$$

- In density estimation, the unknown parameter is probability density itself. The loss function is typically chosen to be a norm in an appropriate function space. For example, for L^2 norm,

$$L(f, \hat{f}) = \|f - \hat{f}\|_2^2$$

the _____ function becomes the mean integrated squared error

$$R(f, \hat{f}) = E\|f - \hat{f}\|^2$$

a. Financial modeling
c. Linear model
b. Risk
d. Risk aversion

16. _____ is one of the four elements of marketing mix. An organization or set of organizations (go-betweens) involved in the process of making a product or service available for use or consumption by a consumer or business user.

The other three parts of the marketing mix are product, pricing, and promotion.

a. Missing completely at random
c. Matching theory
b. Job creation programs
d. Distribution

17. _____ stands for all operations related to the reuse of products and materials. It is 'the process of planning, implementing, and controlling the efficient, cost effective flow of raw materials, in-process inventory, finished goods and related information from the point of consumption to the point of origin for the purpose of recapturing value or proper disposal. More precisely, _____ is the process of moving goods from their typical final destination for the purpose of capturing value, or proper disposal.

a. 33 Strategies of War
c. 1990 Clean Air Act
b. Reverse logistics
d. 28-hour day

18. _____ describes commerce transactions between businesses, such as between a manufacturer and a wholesaler, or between a wholesaler and a retailer. Contrasting terms are business-to-consumer (B2C) and business-to-government (B2G.)

Chapter 11. Supply Chain Management

The volume of B2B transactions is much higher than the volume of B2C transactions.

a. Market environment
c. Product bundling
b. Business-to-business
d. Category management

19. _____ refers to the structured transmission of data between organizations by electronic means. It is used to transfer electronic documents from one computer system to another (ie) from one trading partner to another trading partner. It is more than mere E-mail; for instance, organizations might replace bills of lading and even checks with appropriate _____ messages.

a. A4e
c. Electronic data interchange
b. A Stake in the Outcome
d. AAAI

20. _____ is the application of the management practice of project management to the creation and development of festivals and events.

_____ involves studying the intricacies of the brand, identifying the target audience, devising the event concept, planning the logistics and coordinating the technical aspects before actually executing the modalities of the proposed event.

The recent growth of festivals and events as an industry around the world means that the management can no longer be ad hoc.

a. Energy Management Software
c. Entertainment Management
b. Event management
d. Engineering management

21. _____-model (SCOR(r)) is a process reference model developed by the management consulting firm PRTM and AMR Research and endorsed by the Supply-Chain Council (SCC) as the cross-industry de facto standard diagnostic tool for supply chain management. SCOR enables users to address, improve, and communicate supply chain management practices within and between all interested parties in the Extended Enterprise.

SCOR(r) is a management tool, spanning from the supplier's supplier to the customer's customer. The model has been developed by the members of the Council on a volunteer basis to describe the business activities associated with all phases of satisfying a customer's demand.

a. Supply chain management software
c. Delayed differentiation
b. Supply Chain Risk Management
d. Supply-Chain Operations Reference

22. _____ is the use of an object (typically referred to as an RFID tag) applied to or incorporated into a product, animal, or person for the purpose of identification and tracking using radio waves. Some tags can be read from several meters away and beyond the line of sight of the reader.

Most RFID tags contain at least two parts.

Chapter 11. Supply Chain Management

a. 28-hour day
c. 33 Strategies of War
b. 1990 Clean Air Act
d. Radio-frequency identification

23. A _____ is a type of business entity in which partners (owners) share with each other the profits or losses of the business. _____s are often favored over corporations for taxation purposes, as the _____ structure does not generally incur a tax on profits before it is distributed to the partners (i.e. there is no dividend tax levied.) However, depending on the _____ structure and the jurisdiction in which it operates, owners of a _____ may be exposed to greater personal liability than they would as shareholders of a corporation.

a. Partnership
c. Federal Employers Liability Act
b. Mediation
d. Due process

24. _____ is a practice in logistics of unloading materials from an incoming semi-trailer truck or rail car and loading these materials directly into outbound trucks, trailers with little or no storage in between. This may be done to change type of conveyance, to sort material intended for different destinations or similar destination.

Cross-Dock operations were first pioneered in the US trucking industry in the 1930's, and have been in continuous use in LTL (less than truckload) operations ever since.

a. Product life cycle
c. Small business
b. Corporate recovery
d. Cross-docking

25. _____ or Postponement is a concept in supply chain management where the manufacturing process starts by making a generic or family product that is later differentiated into a specific end-product. This is a widely used method, especially in industries with high demand uncertainty, and can be effectively used to address the final demand even if forecasts cannot be improved.

An example would be Benetton and their knitted sweaters that are initially all white, and then dyed into different colors only when the season/customer color preference/demand is known.

a. Materials management
c. Delayed differentiation
b. Supply-Chain Operations Reference
d. Demand chain

26. In economics, _____ is the removal of intermediaries in a supply chain: 'cutting out the middleman'. Instead of going through traditional distribution channels, which had some type of intermediate (such as a distributor, wholesaler, broker, or agent), companies may now deal with every customer directly, for example via the Internet. One important factor is a drop in the cost of servicing customers directly.

a. Virtual enterprise
c. 28-hour day
b. Disintermediation
d. 1990 Clean Air Act

27. _____ is an operational activity which does an aggregate plan for the production process, in advance of 2 to 18 months, to give an idea to management as to what quantity of materials and other resources are to be procured and when, so that the total cost of operations of the organization is kept to the minimum over that period.

The quantity of outsourcing, subcontracting of items, overtime of labor, numbers to be hired and fired in each period and the amount of inventory to be held in stock and to be backlogged for each period are decided. All of these activities are done within the framework of the company ethics, policies, and long term commitment to the society, community and the country of operation.

a. A Stake in the Outcome
b. Earned value management
c. Earned Schedule
d. Aggregate planning

28. A _____ is a business that is privately owned and operated, with a small number of employees and relatively low volume of sales. The legal definition of 'small' often varies by country and industry, but is generally under 100 employees in the United States and under 50 employees in the European Union. In comparison, the definition of mid-sized business by the number of employees is generally under 500 in the U.S. and 250 for the European Union.
a. Golden Boot Compensation
b. Critical Success Factor
c. Pre-determined overhead rate
d. Small business

29. A _____ is a commercial document issued by a buyer to a seller, indicating types, quantities, and agreed prices for products or services the seller will provide to the buyer. Sending a _____ to a supplier constitutes a legal offer to buy products or services. Acceptance of a _____ by a seller usually forms a one-off contract between the buyer and seller, so no contract exists until the _____ is accepted.
a. 28-hour day
b. Purchase order
c. 1990 Clean Air Act
d. 33 Strategies of War

30. _____ is the management of purchasing process, and related aspects in an organization. Because of production companies purchase nowadays about 70% of their turnover, and service companies purchase approximately 40% of their turnover , _____ is one of the most critical areas in the entire organization and needs intensive management.

Purchasing Process includes as usual 8 main stages as follows:

1. Requisitioning
2. Approving
3. Studying Market
4. Making Purchase Decision
5. Placing Orders
6. Receipting Goods and Services Received
7. Accounting Goods and Services
8. Receiving Invoices and Making Payment
9. Debit note in case of material defect

_____ Process consists usually of 3 stages:

1. Purchasing Planning
2. Purchasing Tracking
3. Purchasing Reporting

Purchasing Planning may include steps as follows:

- creating purchasing projects and tasks
- providing related information (files, links, notes etc.)
- assigning purchasing tasks to employees
- setting task priorities, start/finish dates etc.
- assigning supervisors
- setting reminders

Purchasing Tracking consists of:

- checking task's status and/or history of changes
- receiving status notifications
- sorting, grouping or filtering tasks by current status
- highlighting overdue tasks

Purchasing Reporting includes:

- comparing actual and estimated values
- calculating purchasing task and project statistics
- sorting, grouping or filtering tasks by attributes
- creating charts to visualize key statistics and KPIs

a. Catfish effect
b. Getting Things Done
c. Cross ownership
d. Purchasing Management

31. _____ is the process by which the activities of an organisation, particularly those regarding decision-making, become concentrated within a particular location and/or group.
   a. Corner office
   b. Centralization
   c. Product innovation
   d. Chief operating officer

32. _____ can be regarded as an outcome of mental processes (cognitive process) leading to the selection of a course of action among several alternatives. Every _____ process produces a final choice. The output can be an action or an opinion of choice.
   a. Decision making
   b. 1990 Clean Air Act
   c. 33 Strategies of War
   d. 28-hour day

33. The general definition of an _____ is an evaluation of a person, organization, system, process, project or product. _____s are performed to ascertain the validity and reliability of information; also to provide an assessment of a system's internal control. The goal of an _____ is to express an opinion on the person / organization/system (etc) in question, under evaluation based on work done on a test basis.

a. A Stake in the Outcome
c. Audit committee

b. Internal control
d. Audit

34. _____ is a family of standards for quality management systems. _____ is maintained by ISO, the International Organization for Standardization and is administered by accreditation and certification bodies. The rules are updated, the time and changes in the requirements for quality, motivate change.

a. ISO 9000
c. A4e

b. AAAI
d. A Stake in the Outcome

35. In business management, _____ is money spent to keep and maintain a stock of goods in storage.

The most obvious _____s include rent for the required space; equipment, materials, and labor to operate the space; insurance; security; interest on money invested in the inventory and space, and other direct expenses. Some stored goods become obsolete before they are sold, reducing their contribution to revenue while having no effect on their _____.

a. Choquet integral
c. Private placement

b. Market niche
d. Holding cost

36. The _____ is the level of inventory when a fresh order should be made with suppliers to bring the inventory up by the Economic order quantity ('EOQ'.)

The _____ for replenishment of stock occurs when the level of inventory drops down to zero. In view of instantaneous replenishment of stock the level of inventory jumps to the original level from zero level.

a. Reorder point
c. 1990 Clean Air Act

b. 28-hour day
d. Finished goods

Chapter 12. Inventory Management

1. _____ is a business function that provides a response to customer order enquiries, based on resource availability. It generates available quantities of the requested product, and delivery due dates. Therefore, _____ supports order promising and fulfillment, aiming to manage demand and match it to production plans.
    a. A4e
    b. A Stake in the Outcome
    c. Available-to-promise
    d. AAAI

2. Manufacturing Resource Planning (_____) is defined by APICS as a method for the effective planning of all resources of a manufacturing company. Ideally, it addresses operational planning in units, financial planning in dollars, and has a simulation capability to answer 'what-if' questions and extension of closed-loop MRP. Manufacturing Resource Planning (or MRP2) - Around 1980, over-frequent changes in sales forecasts, entailing continual readjustments in production, as well as the unsuitability of the parameters fixed by the system, led MRP (Material Requirement Planning) to evolve into a new concept : Manufacturing Resource Planning (e.g. MRP 2)

This is not exclusively a software function, but a marriage of people skills, dedication to data base accuracy, and computer resources.

    a. Jidoka
    b. Manufacturing resource planning
    c. Homeworkers
    d. MRP II

3. _____ is a software based production planning and inventory control system used to manage manufacturing processes. Although it is not common nowadays, it is possible to conduct _____ by hand as well.

An _____ system is intended to simultaneously meet three objectives:

- Ensure materials and products are available for production and delivery to customers.
- Maintain the lowest possible level of inventory.
- Plan manufacturing activities, delivery schedules and purchasing activities.

Manufacturing organizations, whatever their products, face the same daily practical problem - that customers want products to be available in a shorter time than it takes to make them. This means that some level of planning is required.

    a. 1990 Clean Air Act
    b. Material requirements planning
    c. 33 Strategies of War
    d. 28-hour day

4. _____ is one of the four Ps of the marketing mix. The other three aspects are product, promotion, and place. It is also a key variable in microeconomic price allocation theory.
    a. Transfer pricing
    b. Penetration pricing
    c. Price floor
    d. Pricing

5. _____ is a term used by inventory specialists to describe a level of extra stock that is maintained below the cycle stock to buffer against stockouts. _____ exists to counter uncertainties in supply and demand. _____ is defined as extra units of inventory carried as protection against possible stockouts .(shortfall in raw material or packaging.)
    a. Product life cycle
    b. Safety stock
    c. Process automation
    d. Knowledge worker

6. A _____ is a list of the general tasks and responsibilities of a position. Typically, it also includes to whom the position reports, specifications such as the qualifications needed by the person in the job, salary range for the position, etc. A _____ is usually developed by conducting a job analysis, which includes examining the tasks and sequences of tasks necessary to perform the job.

   a. Recruitment Process Insourcing
   b. Recruitment advertising
   c. Recruitment
   d. Job description

7. A _____ is a form of direct action, where a group of workers whose jobs are under threat resolve to remain in their place of employment and continue producing without pay. The intention is usually to show that their place of work still has long-term viability, or can be effectively self-managed by the workers.

Historical examples of the _____ include:

- The Upper Clyde Shipbuilders _____ of 1971.
- The Harco Steel _____ of 1971.

   a. Work-in
   b. 28-hour day
   c. Wildcat strike action
   d. 1990 Clean Air Act

8. _____, a business term, is a measure of how products and services supplied by a company meet or surpass customer expectation. It is seen as a key performance indicator within business and is part of the four perspectives of a Balanced Scorecard.

In a competitive marketplace where businesses compete for customers, _____ is seen as a key differentiator and increasingly has become a key element of business strategy.

   a. Horizontal integration
   b. Critical Success Factor
   c. Foreign ownership
   d. Customer satisfaction

9. _____ is the level of inventory that minimizes the total inventory holding costs and ordering costs. The framework used to determine this order quantity is also known as Wilson _____ Model. The model was developed by F. W. Harris in 1913.

   a. Effective executive
   b. Anti-leadership
   c. Event management
   d. Economic order quantity

10. The _____ is an equation that equals the cost of goods sold divided by the average inventory. Average inventory equals beginning inventory plus ending inventory divided by 2.

The formula for _____:

Chapter 12. Inventory Management

The formula for average inventory:

A low turnover rate may point to overstocking, obsolescence, or deficiencies in the product line or marketing effort.

a. Asset turnover
c. A4e
b. A Stake in the Outcome
d. Inventory turnover

11. In a human resources context, _____ or labor _____ is the rate at which an employer gains and loses employees. Simple ways to describe it are 'how long employees tend to stay' or 'the rate of traffic through the revolving door.' _____ is measured for individual companies and for their industry as a whole. If an employer is said to have a high _____ relative to its competitors, it means that employees of that company have a shorter average tenure than those of other companies in the same industry.

a. Turnover
c. Ten year occupational employment projection
b. Continuous
d. Career portfolios

12. _____ is the use of an object (typically referred to as an RFID tag) applied to or incorporated into a product, animal, or person for the purpose of identification and tracking using radio waves. Some tags can be read from several meters away and beyond the line of sight of the reader.

Most RFID tags contain at least two parts.

a. 1990 Clean Air Act
c. Radio-frequency identification
b. 33 Strategies of War
d. 28-hour day

13. The _____ is a barcode symbology (i.e., a specific type of barcode), that is widely used in the United States and Canada for tracking trade items in stores. In the _____-A barcode, each digit is represented by a seven-bit sequence, encoded by a series of alternating bars and spaces. Guard bars, shown in green, separate the two groups of six digits.

The _____ encodes 12 decimal digits as SLLLLLLMRRRRRRE, where S (start) and E (end) are the bit pattern 101, M (middle) is the bit pattern 01010 (called guard bars), and each L (left) and R (right) are digits, each one represented by a seven-bit code.

a. A Stake in the Outcome
c. Universal Product Code
b. AAAI
d. A4e

14. In economics, business, retail, and accounting, a _____ is the value of money that has been used up to produce something, and hence is not available for use anymore. In economics, a _____ is an alternative that is given up as a result of a decision. In business, the _____ may be one of acquisition, in which case the amount of money expended to acquire it is counted as _____.

Chapter 12. Inventory Management

a. Cost overrun
b. Fixed costs
c. Cost allocation
d. Cost

15. The _____ is a systematic, interactive forecasting method which relies on a panel of independent experts. The carefully selected experts answer questionnaires in two or more rounds. After each round, a facilitator provides an anonymous summary of the experts' forecasts from the previous round as well as the reasons they provided for their judgments.
   a. Hoshin Kanri
   b. Quality function deployment
   c. Learning organization
   d. Delphi method

16. In economics, _____ is the desire to own something and the ability to pay for it. The term _____ signifies the ability or the willingness to buy a particular commodity at a given point of time.
   a. 28-hour day
   b. Demand
   c. 1990 Clean Air Act
   d. 33 Strategies of War

17. In business management, _____ is money spent to keep and maintain a stock of goods in storage.

The most obvious _____s include rent for the required space; equipment, materials, and labor to operate the space; insurance; security; interest on money invested in the inventory and space, and other direct expenses. Some stored goods become obsolete before they are sold, reducing their contribution to revenue while having no effect on their _____.

   a. Market niche
   b. Choquet integral
   c. Private placement
   d. Holding cost

18. _____ is an operational activity which does an aggregate plan for the production process, in advance of 2 to 18 months, to give an idea to management as to what quantity of materials and other resources are to be procured and when, so that the total cost of operations of the organization is kept to the minimum over that period.

The quantity of outsourcing, subcontracting of items, overtime of labor, numbers to be hired and fired in each period and the amount of inventory to be held in stock and to be backlogged for each period are decided. All of these activities are done within the framework of the company ethics, policies, and long term commitment to the society, community and the country of operation.

   a. Earned value management
   b. A Stake in the Outcome
   c. Earned Schedule
   d. Aggregate planning

19. _____ is the process of estimation in unknown situations. Prediction is a similar, but more general term. Both can refer to estimation of time series, cross-sectional or longitudinal data.
   a. 33 Strategies of War
   b. 1990 Clean Air Act
   c. 28-hour day
   d. Forecasting

20. A _____ is the period of time between the initiation of any process of production and the completion of that process. Thus the _____ for ordering a new car from a manufacturer may be anywhere from 2 weeks to 6 months. In industry, _____ reduction is an important part of lean manufacturing.

Chapter 12. Inventory Management

a. Lead time
b. 28-hour day
c. 33 Strategies of War
d. 1990 Clean Air Act

21. _____ model is an extension of the Economic Order Quantity model. The _____ model was developed by E.W. Taft in 1918. The difference being that the _____ model assumes orders are received incrementally during the production process.

a. Economic production quantity
b. A Stake in the Outcome
c. A4e
d. Economies of scope

22. The _____ is the level of inventory when a fresh order should be made with suppliers to bring the inventory up by the Economic order quantity ('EOQ'.)

The _____ for replenishment of stock occurs when the level of inventory drops down to zero. In view of instantaneous replenishment of stock the level of inventory jumps to the original level from zero level.

a. Reorder point
b. 28-hour day
c. Finished goods
d. 1990 Clean Air Act

23. _____ is an advertisement in which a particular product specifically mentions a competitor by name for the express purpose of showing why the competitor is inferior to the product naming it.

This should not be confused with parody advertisements, where a fictional product is being advertised for the purpose of poking fun at the particular advertisement, nor should it be confused with the use of a coined brand name for the purpose of comparing the product without actually naming an actual competitor. ('Wikipedia tastes better and is less filling than the Encyclopedia Galactica.')

In the 1980s, during what has been referred to as the cola wars, soft-drink manufacturer Pepsi ran a series of advertisements where people, caught on hidden camera, in a blind taste test, chose Pepsi over rival Coca-Cola.

a. Comparative advertising
b. 28-hour day
c. 1990 Clean Air Act
d. 33 Strategies of War

24. _____ measures the performance of a system. Certain goals are defined and the _____ gives the percentage to which they should be achieved.

Examples

- Percentage of calls answered in a call center.
- Percentage of customers waiting less than a given fixed time.
- Percentage of customers that do not experience a stock out.

_____ is used in supply chain management and in inventory management to measure the performance of inventory systems.

Under stochastic conditions it is unavoidable that in some periods the inventory on hand is not sufficient to deliver the complete demand and, as a consequence, that part of the demand is filled only after an inventory-related waiting time.

a. 1990 Clean Air Act
b. Service level
c. 33 Strategies of War
d. 28-hour day

25. The _____ model is a mathematical model in operations management and applied economics used to determine optimal inventory levels. It is (typically) characterized by fixed prices and uncertain demand. If the inventory level is q, each unit of demand above q is lost.

The standard _____ profit function is:

where D is a random variable representing demand, each unit is sold for price p and purchased for price c, and E is the expectation operator. The solution to the optimal stocking quantity of the _____ is:

where F^{-1} denotes the inverse cumulative distribution function of D.

a. Newsvendor
b. Multiscale decision making
c. 28-hour day
d. 1990 Clean Air Act

26. In probability theory, a probability distribution is called _____ if its cumulative distribution function is _____. This is equivalent to saying that for random variables X with the distribution in question, Pr[X = a] = 0 for all real numbers a, i.e.: the probability that X attains the value a is zero, for any number a. If the distribution of X is _____ then X is called a _____ random variable.

a. Pay Band
b. Continuous
c. Connectionist expert systems
d. Decision tree pruning

Chapter 13. Aggregate Planning

1. _____ is an operational activity which does an aggregate plan for the production process, in advance of 2 to 18 months, to give an idea to management as to what quantity of materials and other resources are to be procured and when, so that the total cost of operations of the organization is kept to the minimum over that period.

The quantity of outsourcing, subcontracting of items, overtime of labor, numbers to be hired and fired in each period and the amount of inventory to be held in stock and to be backlogged for each period are decided. All of these activities are done within the framework of the company ethics, policies, and long term commitment to the society, community and the country of operation.

    a. Earned value management
    b. Earned Schedule
    c. A Stake in the Outcome
    d. Aggregate planning

2. In finance, an _____ is a contract between a buyer and a seller that gives the buyer the right--but not the obligation-- to buy or to sell a particular asset (the underlying asset) at a later day at an agreed price. In return for granting the _____, the seller collects a payment (the premium) from the buyer. A call _____ gives the buyer the right to buy the underlying asset; a put _____ gives the buyer of the _____ the right to sell the underlying asset.

    a. A Stake in the Outcome
    b. A4e
    c. Option
    d. AAAI

3. A _____ is a formal statement of a set of business goals, the reasons why they are believed attainable, and the plan for reaching those goals. It may also contain background information about the organization or team attempting to reach those goals.

The business goals may be defined for for-profit or for non-profit organizations.

    a. Crisis management
    b. Time management
    c. Distributed management
    d. Business plan

4. The _____ is a combinatorial optimization algorithm which solves the assignment problem in polynomial time and which anticipated later primal-dual methods. It was developed and published by Harold Kuhn in 1955, who gave the name '_____' because the algorithm was largely based on the earlier works of two Hungarian mathematicians: D>énes KÅ'nig and JenÅ' Egerv>áry.

James Munkres reviewed the algorithm in 1957 and observed that it is (strongly) polynomial.

    a. 28-hour day
    b. 1990 Clean Air Act
    c. 33 Strategies of War
    d. Hungarian method

5. In economics, _____ is the desire to own something and the ability to pay for it. The term _____ signifies the ability or the willingness to buy a particular commodity at a given point of time.
    a. 28-hour day
    b. Demand
    c. 33 Strategies of War
    d. 1990 Clean Air Act

6. _____ is a concept in economics which refers to the extent to which an enterprise or a nation actually uses its installed productive capacity. Thus, it refers to the relationship between actual output that 'is' produced with the installed equipment and the potential output which 'could' be produced with it, if capacity was fully used.

If market demand grows, _____ will rise.

a. Factors of production
b. Diseconomies of scale
c. Multifactor productivity
d. Capacity utilization

7. _____ or economic opportunity loss is the value of the next best alternative forgone as the result of making a decision. _____ analysis is an important part of a company's decision-making processes but is not treated as an actual cost in any financial statement. The next best thing that a person can engage in is referred to as the _____ of doing the best thing and ignoring the next best thing to be done.

a. AAAI
b. A4e
c. A Stake in the Outcome
d. Opportunity cost

8. _____ is one of the four Ps of the marketing mix. The other three aspects are product, promotion, and place. It is also a key variable in microeconomic price allocation theory.

a. Transfer pricing
b. Price floor
c. Pricing
d. Penetration pricing

9. In economics, business, retail, and accounting, a _____ is the value of money that has been used up to produce something, and hence is not available for use anymore. In economics, a _____ is an alternative that is given up as a result of a decision. In business, the _____ may be one of acquisition, in which case the amount of money expended to acquire it is counted as _____.

a. Cost overrun
b. Cost allocation
c. Fixed costs
d. Cost

10. _____ is a form of communication that typically attempts to persuade potential customers to purchase or to consume more of a particular brand of product or service. 'While now central to the contemporary global economy and the reproduction of global production networks, it is only quite recently that _____ has been more than a marginal influence on patterns of sales and production. The formation of modern _____ was intimately bound up with the emergence of new forms of monopoly capitalism around the end of the 19th and beginning of the 20th century as one element in corporate strategies to create, organize and where possible control markets, especially for mass produced consumer goods.

a. AAAI
b. A Stake in the Outcome
c. A4e
d. Advertising

11. _____ is the amount of time someone works beyond normal working hours. Normal hours may be determined in several ways:

- by custom (what is considered healthy or reasonable by society),
- by practices of a given trade or profession,
- by legislation,
- by agreement between employers and workers or their representatives.

Most nations have _____ laws designed to dissuade or prevent employers from forcing their employees to work excessively long hours. These laws may take into account other considerations than the humanitarian, such as increasing the overall level of employment in the economy. One common approach to regulating _____ is to require employers to pay workers at a higher hourly rate for _____ work.

Chapter 13. Aggregate Planning

a. Organizational structure
b. Industrial relations
c. Organizational effectiveness
d. Overtime

12. The Program (or Project) Evaluation and Review Technique, commonly abbreviated _____, is a model for project management designed to analyze and represent the tasks involved in completing a given project.

_____ is a method to analyze the involved tasks in completing a given project, specially the time needed to complete each task, and identifying the minimum time needed to complete the total project.

_____ was developed primarily to simplify the planning and scheduling of large and complex projects.

a. PERT
b. 33 Strategies of War
c. 1990 Clean Air Act
d. 28-hour day

13. _____ is the temporary suspension or permanent termination of employment of an employee or (more commonly) a group of employees for business reasons, such as the decision that certain positions are no longer necessary or a business slow-down or interruption in work. Originally the term '_____' referred exclusively to a temporary interruption in work, as when factory work cyclically falls off. However, in recent times the term can also refer to the permanent elimination of a position.
   a. Layoff
   b. Wrongful dismissal
   c. Termination of employment
   d. Retirement

14. An _____ is a natural person, business, or corporation which provides goods or services to another entity under terms specified in a contract or within a verbal agreement. Unlike an employee, an _____ does not work regularly for an employer but works as and when required, during which time she or he may be subject to the Law of Agency. _____s are usually paid on a freelance basis.
   a. Equal Pay Act of 1963
   b. Independent contractor
   c. Employment protection legislation
   d. Occupational Safety and Health Act

15. In mathematics, _____ is a technique for optimization of a linear objective function, subject to linear equality and linear inequality constraints. Informally, _____ determines the way to achieve the best outcome (such as maximum profit or lowest cost) in a given mathematical model and given some list of requirements represented as linear equations.

More formally, given a polytope (for example, a polygon or a polyhedron), and a real-valued affine function

$$f(x_1, x_2, \ldots, x_n) = c_1 x_1 + c_2 x_2 + \cdots + c_n x_n + d$$

defined on this polytope, a _____ method will find a point in the polytope where this function has the smallest (or largest) value.

a. Slack variable
b. Linear programming relaxation
c. Linear programming
d. 1990 Clean Air Act

Chapter 13. Aggregate Planning

16. _____ of the learning curve effect and the closely related experience curve effect express the relationship between equations for experience and efficiency or between efficiency gains and investment in the effort. The experience of 'learning curves' was first observed by the 19th Century German psychologist Hermann Ebbinghaus according to the difficulty of memorizing varying numbers of verbal stimuli, and subsequent learning about the complex processes of learning are discussed in the

.

The rule used for representing the learning curve effect states that the more times a task has been performed, the less time will be required on each subsequent iteration.

- a. Distribution
- b. Spatial Decision Support Systems
- c. Point biserial correlation coefficient
- d. Models

17. _____ is an advertisement in which a particular product specifically mentions a competitor by name for the express purpose of showing why the competitor is inferior to the product naming it.

This should not be confused with parody advertisements, where a fictional product is being advertised for the purpose of poking fun at the particular advertisement, nor should it be confused with the use of a coined brand name for the purpose of comparing the product without actually naming an actual competitor. ('Wikipedia tastes better and is less filling than the Encyclopedia Galactica.')

In the 1980s, during what has been referred to as the cola wars, soft-drink manufacturer Pepsi ran a series of advertisements where people, caught on hidden camera, in a blind taste test, chose Pepsi over rival Coca-Cola.

- a. 28-hour day
- b. 33 Strategies of War
- c. 1990 Clean Air Act
- d. Comparative advertising

18. _____ is the process of understanding, anticipating and influencing consumer behavior in order to maximize revenue or profits from a fixed, perishable resource This process was first discovered by Dr. Matt H. Keller. The challenge is to sell the right resources to the right customer at the right time for the right price.

- a. Business networking
- b. Gap analysis
- c. Yield management
- d. Business model design

19. A _____ is a plan for production, staffing, inventory, etc. It is usually linked to manufacturing where the plan indicates when and how much of each product will be demanded. This plan quantifies significant processes, parts, and other resources in order to optimize production, to identify bottlenecks, and to anticipate needs and completed goods.

- a. Value engineering
- b. Piecework
- c. Remanufacturing
- d. Master production schedule

20. _____ is a business function that provides a response to customer order enquiries, based on resource availability. It generates available quantities of the requested product, and delivery due dates. Therefore, _____ supports order promising and fulfillment, aiming to manage demand and match it to production plans.

- a. A4e
- b. A Stake in the Outcome
- c. AAAI
- d. Available-to-promise

21. _____ is the process of determining the production capacity needed by an organization to meet changing demands for its products. In the context of _____, 'capacity' is the maximum amount of work that an organization is capable of completing in a given period of time.

A discrepancy between the capacity of an organization and the demands of its customers results in inefficiency, either in under-utilized resources or unfulfilled customers.

a. Scientific management
c. Remanufacturing
b. Productivity
d. Capacity planning

Chapter 14. MRP and ERP

1. In economics, _____ is the desire to own something and the ability to pay for it. The term _____ signifies the ability or the willingness to buy a particular commodity at a given point of time.
   - a. 33 Strategies of War
   - b. 28-hour day
   - c. 1990 Clean Air Act
   - d. Demand

2. _____ is an operational activity which does an aggregate plan for the production process, in advance of 2 to 18 months, to give an idea to management as to what quantity of materials and other resources are to be procured and when, so that the total cost of operations of the organization is kept to the minimum over that period.

   The quantity of outsourcing, subcontracting of items, overtime of labor, numbers to be hired and fired in each period and the amount of inventory to be held in stock and to be backlogged for each period are decided. All of these activities are done within the framework of the company ethics, policies, and long term commitment to the society, community and the country of operation.

   - a. A Stake in the Outcome
   - b. Earned Schedule
   - c. Aggregate planning
   - d. Earned value management

3. Manufacturing Resource Planning (_____) is defined by APICS as a method for the effective planning of all resources of a manufacturing company. Ideally, it addresses operational planning in units, financial planning in dollars, and has a simulation capability to answer 'what-if' questions and extension of closed-loop MRP. Manufacturing Resource Planning (or MRP2) - Around 1980, over-frequent changes in sales forecasts, entailing continual readjustments in production, as well as the unsuitability of the parameters fixed by the system, led MRP (Material Requirement Planning) to evolve into a new concept : Manufacturing Resource Planning (e.g. MRP 2)

   This is not exclusively a software function, but a marriage of people skills, dedication to data base accuracy, and computer resources.

   - a. MRP II
   - b. Jidoka
   - c. Homeworkers
   - d. Manufacturing resource planning

4. _____ is a software based production planning and inventory control system used to manage manufacturing processes. Although it is not common nowadays, it is possible to conduct _____ by hand as well.

   An _____ system is intended to simultaneously meet three objectives:

   - Ensure materials and products are available for production and delivery to customers.
   - Maintain the lowest possible level of inventory.
   - Plan manufacturing activities, delivery schedules and purchasing activities.

   Manufacturing organizations, whatever their products, face the same daily practical problem - that customers want products to be available in a shorter time than it takes to make them. This means that some level of planning is required.

   - a. 28-hour day
   - b. 33 Strategies of War
   - c. Material requirements planning
   - d. 1990 Clean Air Act

Chapter 14. MRP and ERP

5. The _____ is a combinatorial optimization algorithm which solves the assignment problem in polynomial time and which anticipated later primal-dual methods. It was developed and published by Harold Kuhn in 1955, who gave the name '_____' because the algorithm was largely based on the earlier works of two Hungarian mathematicians: D>énes KÅ'nig and JenÅ' Egerv>áry.

James Munkres reviewed the algorithm in 1957 and observed that it is (strongly) polynomial.

a. 33 Strategies of War
b. 1990 Clean Air Act
c. Hungarian method
d. 28-hour day

6. A _____ is a plan for production, staffing, inventory, etc. It is usually linked to manufacturing where the plan indicates when and how much of each product will be demanded. This plan quantifies significant processes, parts, and other resources in order to optimize production, to identify bottlenecks, and to anticipate needs and completed goods.

a. Piecework
b. Remanufacturing
c. Value engineering
d. Master production schedule

7. _____ is a list of the raw materials, sub-assemblies, intermediate assemblies, sub-components, components, parts and the quantities of each needed to manufacture an end item (final product).

a. Scientific management
b. Bill of materials
c. Methods-time measurement
d. Piece rate

8. A _____ is the period of time between the initiation of any process of production and the completion of that process. Thus the _____ for ordering a new car from a manufacturer may be anywhere from 2 weeks to 6 months. In industry, _____ reduction is an important part of lean manufacturing.

a. 33 Strategies of War
b. Lead time
c. 1990 Clean Air Act
d. 28-hour day

9. _____ is a term used by inventory specialists to describe a level of extra stock that is maintained below the cycle stock to buffer against stockouts. _____ exists to counter uncertainties in supply and demand. _____ is defined as extra units of inventory carried as protection against possible stockouts .(shortfall in raw material or packaging.)

a. Knowledge worker
b. Safety stock
c. Product life cycle
d. Process automation

10. _____ is the level of inventory that minimizes the total inventory holding costs and ordering costs. The framework used to determine this order quantity is also known as Wilson _____ Model. The model was developed by F. W. Harris in 1913.

a. Event management
b. Anti-leadership
c. Effective executive
d. Economic order quantity

11. _____ is an advertisement in which a particular product specifically mentions a competitor by name for the express purpose of showing why the competitor is inferior to the product naming it.

This should not be confused with parody advertisements, where a fictional product is being advertised for the purpose of poking fun at the particular advertisement, nor should it be confused with the use of a coined brand name for the purpose of comparing the product without actually naming an actual competitor. ('Wikipedia tastes better and is less filling than the Encyclopedia Galactica.')

Chapter 14. MRP and ERP

In the 1980s, during what has been referred to as the cola wars, soft-drink manufacturer Pepsi ran a series of advertisements where people, caught on hidden camera, in a blind taste test, chose Pepsi over rival Coca-Cola.

a. 33 Strategies of War
b. 28-hour day
c. 1990 Clean Air Act
d. Comparative advertising

12. _____ is a company-wide computer software system used to manage and coordinate all the resources, information, and functions of a business from shared data stores.

An _____ system has a service-oriented architecture with modular hardware and software units and 'services' that communicate on a local area network. The modular design allows a business to add or reconfigure modules (perhaps from different vendors) while preserving data integrity in one shared database that may be centralized or distributed.

a. Enterprise resource planning
b. A Stake in the Outcome
c. AAAI
d. A4e

13. In economics, and cost accounting, _____ describes the total economic cost of production and is made up of variable costs, which vary according to the quantity of a good produced and include inputs such as labor and raw materials, plus fixed costs, which are independent of the quantity of a good produced and include inputs (capital) that cannot be varied in the short term, such as buildings and machinery. _____ in economics includes the total opportunity cost of each factor of production in addition to fixed and variable costs.

The rate at which _____ changes as the amount produced changes is called marginal cost.

a. 33 Strategies of War
b. 28-hour day
c. Total cost
d. 1990 Clean Air Act

14. _____ is a financial estimate designed to help consumers and enterprise managers assess direct and indirect costs It is a form of full cost accounting.
a. 28-hour day
b. Total cost of ownership
c. 33 Strategies of War
d. 1990 Clean Air Act

15. In economics, business, retail, and accounting, a _____ is the value of money that has been used up to produce something, and hence is not available for use anymore. In economics, a _____ is an alternative that is given up as a result of a decision. In business, the _____ may be one of acquisition, in which case the amount of money expended to acquire it is counted as _____.
a. Cost overrun
b. Fixed costs
c. Cost allocation
d. Cost

16. _____ is the state or fact of exclusive rights and control over property, which may be an object, land/real estate or intellectual property. An _____ right is also referred to as title. The concept of _____ has existed for thousands of years and in all cultures.

a. Emanation of the state
c. A Stake in the Outcome
b. A4e
d. Ownership

17. _____, commonly known as e-commerce, consists of the buying and selling of products or services over electronic systems such as the Internet and other computer networks. The amount of trade conducted electronically has grown extraordinarily with widespread Internet usage. The use of commerce is conducted in this way, spurring and drawing on innovations in electronic funds transfer, supply chain management, Internet marketing, online transaction processing, electronic data interchange (EDI), inventory management systems, and automated data collection systems.

a. A4e
c. Electronic Commerce
b. Online shopping
d. A Stake in the Outcome

18. _____ refers to the movement of cash into or out of a business or financial product. It is usually measured during a specified, finite period of time. Measurement of _____ can be used

- to determine a project's rate of return or value. The time of _____s into and out of projects are used as inputs in financial models such as internal rate of return, and net present value.
- to determine problems with a business's liquidity. Being profitable does not necessarily mean being liquid. A company can fail because of a shortage of cash, even while profitable.
- as an alternate measure of a business's profits when it is believed that accrual accounting concepts do not represent economic realities. For example, a company may be notionally profitable but generating little operational cash (as may be the case for a company that barters its products rather than selling for cash.) In such a case, the company may be deriving additional operating cash by issuing shares evaluating default risk, re-investment requirements, etc.

_____ is a generic term used differently depending on the context. It may be defined by users for their own purposes.

a. Gross profit margin
c. Sweat equity
b. Gross profit
d. Cash flow

Chapter 15. JIT and Lean Operations

1. _____ is an inventory strategy that strives to improve the return on investment of a business by reducing in-process inventory and its associated carrying costs. To meet _____ objectives, the process relies on signals between different points in the process. This means the process is often driven by a series of signals, or Kanban , which tell production when to make the next part. Kanban are usually 'tickets' but can be simple visual signals, such as the presence or absence of a part on a shelf. Implemented correctly, _____ can dramatically improve a manufacturing organization's return on investment, quality, and efficiency.
   a. 33 Strategies of War
   b. 28-hour day
   c. 1990 Clean Air Act
   d. Just-in-time

2. Autonomation describes a feature of machine design to effect the principle of _____ used in the Toyota Production System (TPS) and Lean manufacturing. It may be described as 'intelligent automation' or 'automation with a human touch.' This type of automation implements some supervisory functions rather than production functions. At Toyota this usually means that if an abnormal situation arises the machine stops and the worker will stop the production line.
   a. Homeworkers
   b. Manufacturing resource planning
   c. MRP II
   d. Jidoka

3. _____ is a Japanese philosophy that focuses on continuous improvement throughout all aspects of life. When applied to the workplace, _____ activities continually improve all functions of a business, from manufacturing to management and from the CEO to the assembly line workers. By improving standardized activities and processes, _____ aims to eliminate waste .
   a. Cross-docking
   b. Psychological pricing
   c. Kaizen
   d. Sensitivity analysis

4. _____ is a concept related to lean and just-in-time (JIT) production. The Japanese word _____ is a common term meaning 'signboard' or 'billboard'. According to Taiichi Ohno, the man credited with developing JIT, _____ is a means through which JIT is achieved.
   a. Succession planning
   b. Risk management
   c. Trademark
   d. Kanban

5. _____ is a Japanese term that means 'fail-safing' or 'mistake-proofing'. A _____ is any mechanism in a Lean manufacturing process that helps an equipment operator avoid (yokeru) mistakes (poka.) Its purpose is to eliminate product defects by preventing, correcting, or drawing attention to human errors as they occur.
   a. 28-hour day
   b. 33 Strategies of War
   c. 1990 Clean Air Act
   d. Poka-yoke

6. In organizational development (OD), _____ is a series of actions taken by a Process Owner to identify, analyze and improve existing processes within an organization to meet new goals and objectives. These actions often follow a specific methodology or strategy to create successful results. A sampling of these are listed below.
   a. Letter of resignation
   b. Supervisory board
   c. Product innovation
   d. Process improvement

7. _____ is a work methodology based on the parallelization of tasks (ie. concurrently.) It refers to an approach used in product development in which functions of design engineering, manufacturing engineering and other functions are integrated to reduce the elapsed time required to bring a new product to the market.
   a. Project management
   b. Concurrent engineering
   c. Work package
   d. Critical Chain Project Management

Chapter 15. JIT and Lean Operations

8. In systems engineering, _____ is an approach that subdivides a system into smaller parts (modules) that can be independently created and then used in different systems to drive multiple functionalities. Besides reduction in cost (due to lesser customization, and less learning time), and flexibility in design, modularity offers other benefits such as augmentation (adding new solution by merely plugging in a new module), and exclusion. Examples of modular systems are cars, computers and high rise buildings.
   a. Statement of work
   b. 28-hour day
   c. 1990 Clean Air Act
   d. Modular design

9. _____ is used for the design, development, analysis, and optimization of technical processes and is mainly applied to chemical plants and chemical processes, but also to power stations, and similar technical facilities. Process flow diagram of a typical amine treating process used in industrial plants

_____ is a model-based representation of chemical, physical, biological, and other technical processes and unit operations in software. Basic prerequisites are a thorough knowledge of chemical and physical properties of pure components and mixtures, of reactions, and of mathematical models which, in combination, allow the calculation of a process in computers.

   a. 33 Strategies of War
   b. 1990 Clean Air Act
   c. 28-hour day
   d. Process simulation

10. _____ can be defined as the idea generation, concept development, testing and manufacturing or implementation of a physical object or service. _____ers conceptualize and evaluate ideas, making them tangible through products in a more systematic approach. The role of a _____er encompasses many characteristics of the marketing manager, product manager, industrial designer and design engineer.
   a. Product design
   b. Affiliation
   c. Abraham Harold Maslow
   d. Adam Smith

11. _____ is an advertisement in which a particular product specifically mentions a competitor by name for the express purpose of showing why the competitor is inferior to the product naming it.

This should not be confused with parody advertisements, where a fictional product is being advertised for the purpose of poking fun at the particular advertisement, nor should it be confused with the use of a coined brand name for the purpose of comparing the product without actually naming an actual competitor. ('Wikipedia tastes better and is less filling than the Encyclopedia Galactica.')

In the 1980s, during what has been referred to as the cola wars, soft-drink manufacturer Pepsi ran a series of advertisements where people, caught on hidden camera, in a blind taste test, chose Pepsi over rival Coca-Cola.

   a. 1990 Clean Air Act
   b. Comparative advertising
   c. 33 Strategies of War
   d. 28-hour day

12. _____ is the level of inventory that minimizes the total inventory holding costs and ordering costs. The framework used to determine this order quantity is also known as Wilson _____ Model. The model was developed by F. W. Harris in 1913.

Chapter 15. JIT and Lean Operations

a. Anti-leadership
c. Effective executive
b. Event management
d. Economic order quantity

13. _____ is one of the many lean production methods for reducing waste in a manufacturing process. It provides a rapid and efficient way of converting a manufacturing process from running the current product to running the next product. This rapid changeover is key to reducing production lot sizes and thereby improving flow ' href='/wiki/Mura_'>Mura) The phrase 'single minute' does not mean that all changeovers and startups should take only one minute, but that they should take less than 10 minutes (in other words, 'single digit minute'.)

a. Process capability
c. Quality control
b. Single Minute Exchange of Die
d. Statistical process control

14. The metastability in flip-flops can be avoided by ensuring that the data and control inputs are held valid and constant for specified periods before and after the clock pulse, called the _____ and the hold time (t_h) respectively. These times are specified in the data sheet for the device, and are typically between a few nanoseconds and a few hundred picoseconds for modern devices.

Unfortunately, it is not always possible to meet the setup and hold criteria, because the flip-flop may be connected to a real-time signal that could change at any time, outside the control of the designer.

a. 33 Strategies of War
c. 1990 Clean Air Act
b. 28-hour day
d. Setup time

15. _____ describes a feature of machine design to effect the principle of jidoka (è‡ªåƒ åŒ–) used in the Toyota Production System (TPS) and Lean manufacturing. It may be described as 'intelligent automation' or 'automation with a human touch.' This type of automation implements some supervisory functions rather than production functions. At Toyota this usually means that if an abnormal situation arises the machine stops and the worker will stop the production line.

a. AAAI
c. Autonomation
b. A Stake in the Outcome
d. A4e

16. In engineering and manufacturing, _____ and quality engineering are used in developing systems to ensure products or services are designed and produced to meet or exceed customer requirements. Refer to the definition by Merriam-Webster for further information . These systems are often developed in conjunction with other business and engineering disciplines using a cross-functional approach.

a. Statistical process control
c. Single Minute Exchange of Die
b. Process capability
d. Quality control

17. _____ can be defined as the maximum time per unit allowed to produce a product in order to meet demand. It is derived from the German word Taktzeit which translates to cycle time. _____ sets the pace for industrial manufacturing lines. In automobile manufacturing, for example, cars are assembled on a line, and are moved on to the next station after a certain time - the _____. Therefore, the time needed to complete work on each station has to be less than the _____ in order for the product to be completed within the alloted time.

a. Production line
c. Takt time
b. Six Sigma
d. Theory of constraints

18. _____ is one of the managerial functions like planning, organizing, staffing and directing. It is an important function because it helps to check the errors and to take the corrective action so that deviation from standards are minimized and stated goals of the organization are achieved in desired manner. According to modern concepts, _____ is a foreseeing action whereas earlier concept of _____ was used only when errors were detected. _____ in management means setting standards, measuring actual performance and taking corrective action.
   a. Schedule of reinforcement
   b. Decision tree pruning
   c. Turnover
   d. Control

19. Quality management can be considered to have three main components: quality control, quality assurance and _____. Quality management is focused not only on product quality, but also the means to achieve it. Quality management therefore uses quality assurance and control of processes as well as products to achieve more consistent quality.
   a. Quality management
   b. 1990 Clean Air Act
   c. 28-hour day
   d. Quality improvement

20. _____ is a business function that provides a response to customer order enquiries, based on resource availability. It generates available quantities of the requested product, and delivery due dates. Therefore, _____ supports order promising and fulfillment, aiming to manage demand and match it to production plans.
   a. A Stake in the Outcome
   b. A4e
   c. AAAI
   d. Available-to-promise

21. A _____ is a form of direct action, where a group of workers whose jobs are under threat resolve to remain in their place of employment and continue producing without pay. The intention is usually to show that their place of work still has long-term viability, or can be effectively self-managed by the workers.

   Historical examples of the _____ include:

   - The Upper Clyde Shipbuilders _____ of 1971.
   - The Harco Steel _____ of 1971.

   a. 1990 Clean Air Act
   b. 28-hour day
   c. Wildcat strike action
   d. Work-in

22. In probability theory, a probability distribution is called _____ if its cumulative distribution function is _____. This is equivalent to saying that for random variables X with the distribution in question, Pr[X = a] = 0 for all real numbers a, i.e.: the probability that X attains the value a is zero, for any number a. If the distribution of X is _____ then X is called a _____ random variable.
   a. Pay Band
   b. Decision tree pruning
   c. Connectionist expert systems
   d. Continuous

23. _____ is a management process whereby delivery (customer valued) processes are constantly evaluated and improved in the light of their efficiency, effectiveness and flexibility.

Some see it as a meta process for most management systems (Business Process Management, Quality Management, Project Management). Deming saw it as part of the 'system' whereby feedback from the process and customer were evaluated against organisational goals.

a. First-mover advantage
b. Critical Success Factor
c. Sole proprietorship
d. Continuous Improvement Process

24. A _____ is a process in which a potential employee is evaluated by an employer for prospective employment in their company, organization and was established in the late 16th century.

A _____ typically precedes the hiring decision, and is used to evaluate the candidate. The interview is usually preceded by the evaluation of submitted résumés from interested candidates, then selecting a small number of candidates for interviews.

a. Split shift
b. Payrolling
c. Supported employment
d. Job interview

25. The _____ captures an expanded spectrum of values and criteria for measuring organizational success: economic, ecological and social. With the ratification of the United Nations and ICLEI _____ standard for urban and community accounting in early 2007, this became the dominant approach to public sector full cost accounting. Similar UN standards apply to natural capital and human capital measurement to assist in measurements required by _____, e.g. the ecoBudget standard for reporting ecological footprint.

a. 33 Strategies of War
b. 1990 Clean Air Act
c. Triple bottom line
d. 28-hour day

26. In business and accounting, _____s are everything of value that is owned by a person or company. Any property or object of value that one possesses, usually considered as applicable to the payment of one's debts is considered an _____. Simplistically stated, _____s are things of value that can be readily converted into cash.

a. AAAI
b. A Stake in the Outcome
c. A4e
d. Asset

27. _____ is a costing model that identifies activities in an organization and assigns the cost of each activity resource to all products and services according to the actual consumption by each: it assigns more indirect costs (overhead) into direct costs.

In this way an organization can establish the true cost of its individual products and services for the purposes of identifying and eliminating those which are unprofitable and lowering the prices of those which are overpriced.

In a business organization, the ABC methodology assigns an organization's resource costs through activities to the products and services provided to its customers.

a. Activity-based costing
b. Indirect costs
c. A4e
d. A Stake in the Outcome

Chapter 15. JIT and Lean Operations

28. In economics, business, retail, and accounting, a _____ is the value of money that has been used up to produce something, and hence is not available for use anymore. In economics, a _____ is an alternative that is given up as a result of a decision. In business, the _____ may be one of acquisition, in which case the amount of money expended to acquire it is counted as _____.
    a. Cost
    b. Fixed costs
    c. Cost overrun
    d. Cost allocation

29. In management accounting, _____ establishes budget and actual cost of operations, processes, departments or product and the analysis of variances, profitability or social use of funds. Managers use _____ to support decision-making to cut a company's costs and improve profitability. As a form of management accounting, _____ need not follow standards such as GAAP, because its primary use is for internal managers, rather than outside users, and what to compute is instead decided pragmatically.
    a. Cost accounting
    b. Marginal cost
    c. Quality costs
    d. Transaction cost

30. _____ has been described as the 'process of social influence in which one person can enlist the aid and support of others in the accomplishment of a common task' . A definition more inclusive of followers comes from Alan Keith of Genentech who said '_____ is ultimately about creating a way for people to contribute to making something extraordinary happen.'

    _____ is one of the most salient aspects of the organizational context. However, defining _____ has been challenging.

    a. Leadership
    b. Situational leadership
    c. 1990 Clean Air Act
    d. 28-hour day

31. In business, overhead, _____ or overhead expense refers to an ongoing expense of operating a business. The term overhead is usually used to group expenses that are necessary to the continued functioning of the business, but do not directly generate profits.

    Overhead expenses are all costs on the income statement except for direct labor and direct materials.

    a. Industrial market segmentation
    b. Intangible assets
    c. Overhead cost
    d. Interlocking directorate

32. _____ has the following meanings:

    The care and servicing by personnel for the purpose of maintaining equipment and facilities in satisfactory operating condition by providing for systematic inspection, detection, and correction of incipient failures either before they occur or before they develop into major defects.

    1. Maintenance, including tests, measurements, adjustments, and parts replacement, performed specifically to prevent faults from occurring.

While _____ is generally considered to be worthwhile, there are risks such as equipment failure or human error involved when performing _____, just as in any maintenance operation. _____ as scheduled overhaul or scheduled replacement provides two of the three proactive failure management policies available to the maintenance engineer. Common methods of determining what _____ failure management policies should be applied are; OEM recommendations, requirements of codes and legislation within a jurisdiction, what an 'expert' thinks ought to be done, or the maintenance that's already done to similar equipment.

a. 28-hour day
b. 33 Strategies of War
c. Preventive maintenance
d. 1990 Clean Air Act

33. _____ is a family of business models in which the buyer of a product provides certain information to a supplier of that product and the supplier takes full responsibility for maintaining an agreed inventory of the material, usually at the buyer's consumption location (usually a store.) A third party logistics provider can also be involved to make sure that the buyer has the required level of inventory by adjusting the demand and supply gaps.

As a symbiotic relationship, _____ makes it less likely that a business will unintentionally become out of stock of a good and reduces inventory in the supply chain.

a. Vendor Managed Inventory
b. Delayed differentiation
c. Supply Chain Risk Management
d. Supply-Chain Operations Reference

34. A _____ is a computer program typically used to provide some form of artificial intelligence, which consists primarily of a set of rules about behavior. These rules, termed productions, are a basic representation found useful in AI planning, expert systems and action selection. A _____ provides the mechanism necessary to execute productions in order to achieve some goal for the system.

a. 28-hour day
b. Production system
c. 1990 Clean Air Act
d. 33 Strategies of War

35. _____ techniques help determine the condition of in-service equipment in order to predict when maintenance should be performed. This approach offers cost savings over routine or time-based preventive maintenance, because tasks are performed only when warranted.

PdM, or condition-based maintenance, attempts to evaluate the condition of equipment by performing periodic or continuous (online) equipment condition monitoring.

a. Reverse engineering
b. 1990 Clean Air Act
c. 28-hour day
d. Predictive maintenance

Chapter 16. Scheduling

1. A _____ is a type of bar chart that illustrates a project schedule. _____s illustrate the start and finish dates of the terminal elements and summary elements of a project. Terminal elements and summary elements comprise the work breakdown structure of the project.
   - a. 33 Strategies of War
   - b. 28-hour day
   - c. Gantt chart
   - d. 1990 Clean Air Act

2. The _____ is a combinatorial optimization algorithm which solves the assignment problem in polynomial time and which anticipated later primal-dual methods. It was developed and published by Harold Kuhn in 1955, who gave the name '_____' because the algorithm was largely based on the earlier works of two Hungarian mathematicians: D>énes KÅ'nig and JenÅ' Egerv>áry.

   James Munkres reviewed the algorithm in 1957 and observed that it is (strongly) polynomial.

   - a. 33 Strategies of War
   - b. 28-hour day
   - c. 1990 Clean Air Act
   - d. Hungarian method

3. The metastability in flip-flops can be avoided by ensuring that the data and control inputs are held valid and constant for specified periods before and after the clock pulse, called the _____ and the hold time (t_h) respectively. These times are specified in the data sheet for the device, and are typically between a few nanoseconds and a few hundred picoseconds for modern devices.

   Unfortunately, it is not always possible to meet the setup and hold criteria, because the flip-flop may be connected to a real-time signal that could change at any time, outside the control of the designer.

   - a. 28-hour day
   - b. 33 Strategies of War
   - c. 1990 Clean Air Act
   - d. Setup time

4. In economics, business, retail, and accounting, a _____ is the value of money that has been used up to produce something, and hence is not available for use anymore. In economics, a _____ is an alternative that is given up as a result of a decision. In business, the _____ may be one of acquisition, in which case the amount of money expended to acquire it is counted as _____.
   - a. Fixed costs
   - b. Cost
   - c. Cost overrun
   - d. Cost allocation

5. _____ is one of the managerial functions like planning, organizing, staffing and directing. It is an important function because it helps to check the errors and to take the corrective action so that deviation from standards are minimized and stated goals of the organization are achieved in desired manner.According to modern concepts, _____ is a foreseeing action whereas earlier concept of _____ was used only when errors were detected. _____ in management means setting standards, measuring actual performance and taking corrective action.
   - a. Turnover
   - b. Schedule of reinforcement
   - c. Control
   - d. Decision tree pruning

6. In mathematics, _____ is a technique for optimization of a linear objective function, subject to linear equality and linear inequality constraints. Informally, _____ determines the way to achieve the best outcome (such as maximum profit or lowest cost) in a given mathematical model and given some list of requirements represented as linear equations.

More formally, given a polytope (for example, a polygon or a polyhedron), and a real-valued affine function

$$f(x_1, x_2, \ldots, x_n) = c_1 x_1 + c_2 x_2 + \cdots + c_n x_n + d$$

defined on this polytope, a _____ method will find a point in the polytope where this function has the smallest (or largest) value.

a. 1990 Clean Air Act
b. Linear programming relaxation
c. Slack variable
d. Linear programming

7. The Program (or Project) Evaluation and Review Technique, commonly abbreviated _____, is a model for project management designed to analyze and represent the tasks involved in completing a given project.

_____ is a method to analyze the involved tasks in completing a given project, specially the time needed to complete each task, and identifying the minimum time needed to complete the total project.

_____ was developed primarily to simplify the planning and scheduling of large and complex projects.

a. 1990 Clean Air Act
b. PERT
c. 33 Strategies of War
d. 28-hour day

8. _____ is an overall management philosophy introduced by Dr. Eliyahu M. Goldratt in his 1984 book titled The Goal, that is geared to help organizations continually achieve their goal. The title comes from the contention that any manageable system is limited in achieving more of its goal by a very small number of constraints, and that there is always at least one constraint. The _____ process seeks to identify the constraint and restructure the rest of the organization around it, through the use of the Five Focusing Steps.

a. Six Sigma
b. Theory of constraints
c. Production line
d. Takt time

9. _____ can be regarded as an outcome of mental processes (cognitive process) leading to the selection of a course of action among several alternatives. Every _____ process produces a final choice. The output can be an action or an opinion of choice.

a. 1990 Clean Air Act
b. Decision making
c. 33 Strategies of War
d. 28-hour day

10. _____ ('Plan-Do-Check-Act') is an iterative four-step problem-solving process typically used in business process improvement. It is also known as the Deming Cycle, Shewhart cycle, Deming Wheel, or Plan-Do-Study-Act.

_____ was made popular by Dr. W. Edwards Deming, who is considered by many to be the father of modern quality control; however it was always referred to by him as the Shewhart cycle. Later in Deming's career, he modified _____ to Plan, Do, Study, Act (PDSA) so as to better describe his recommendations.

a. PDCA
b. Decentralization
c. Management team
d. Management by exception

11. _____ is an advertisement in which a particular product specifically mentions a competitor by name for the express purpose of showing why the competitor is inferior to the product naming it.

This should not be confused with parody advertisements, where a fictional product is being advertised for the purpose of poking fun at the particular advertisement, nor should it be confused with the use of a coined brand name for the purpose of comparing the product without actually naming an actual competitor. ('Wikipedia tastes better and is less filling than the Encyclopedia Galactica.')

In the 1980s, during what has been referred to as the cola wars, soft-drink manufacturer Pepsi ran a series of advertisements where people, caught on hidden camera, in a blind taste test, chose Pepsi over rival Coca-Cola.

a. 1990 Clean Air Act
b. 33 Strategies of War
c. 28-hour day
d. Comparative advertising

12. _____ is the process of understanding, anticipating and influencing consumer behavior in order to maximize revenue or profits from a fixed, perishable resource This process was first discovered by Dr. Matt H. Keller. The challenge is to sell the right resources to the right customer at the right time for the right price.
a. Business networking
b. Yield management
c. Gap analysis
d. Business model design

13. The _____ is the labour pool in employment. It is generally used to describe those working for a single company or industry, but can also apply to a geographic region like a city, country, state, etc. The term generally excludes the employers or management, and implies those involved in manual labour.
a. Workforce
b. Division of labour
c. Work-life balance
d. Pink-collar worker

Chapter 17. Project Management

1. _____ refers to the movement of cash into or out of a business or financial product. It is usually measured during a specified, finite period of time. Measurement of _____ can be used

- to determine a project's rate of return or value. The time of _____s into and out of projects are used as inputs in financial models such as internal rate of return, and net present value.
- to determine problems with a business's liquidity. Being profitable does not necessarily mean being liquid. A company can fail because of a shortage of cash, even while profitable.
- as an alternate measure of a business's profits when it is believed that accrual accounting concepts do not represent economic realities. For example, a company may be notionally profitable but generating little operational cash (as may be the case for a company that barters its products rather than selling for cash.) In such a case, the company may be deriving additional operating cash by issuing shares evaluating default risk, re-investment requirements, etc.

_____ is a generic term used differently depending on the context. It may be defined by users for their own purposes.

a. Gross profit
b. Gross profit margin
c. Sweat equity
d. Cash flow

2. _____ is the discipline of planning, organizing and managing resources to bring about the successful completion of specific project goals and objectives. It is often closely related to and sometimes conflated with Program management.

A project is a finite endeavor--having specific start and completion dates--undertaken to meet particular goals and objectives, usually to bring about beneficial change or added value.

a. Project management
b. Precedence diagram
c. Work package
d. Project engineer

3. A _____ is a type of bar chart that illustrates a project schedule. _____s illustrate the start and finish dates of the terminal elements and summary elements of a project. Terminal elements and summary elements comprise the work breakdown structure of the project.

a. 33 Strategies of War
b. 1990 Clean Air Act
c. Gantt chart
d. 28-hour day

4. _____ is a type of organizational management in which people with similar skills are pooled for work assignments. For example, all engineers may be in one engineering department and report to an engineering manager, but these same engineers may be assigned to different projects and report to a project manager while working on that project. Therefore, each engineer may have to work under several managers to get their job done.

a. Management development
b. Matrix management
c. Central Administration
d. Span of control

5. The Program (or Project) Evaluation and Review Technique, commonly abbreviated _____, is a model for project management designed to analyze and represent the tasks involved in completing a given project.

_____ is a method to analyze the involved tasks in completing a given project, specially the time needed to complete each task, and identifying the minimum time needed to complete the total project.

_____ was developed primarily to simplify the planning and scheduling of large and complex projects.

a. 28-hour day
c. 33 Strategies of War
b. 1990 Clean Air Act
d. PERT

6. In decision theory and estimation theory, the _____ of an estimator, $\hat{\theta}$, of an unknown parameter of the distribution, θ, is the expected value of the loss function

$$R(\theta, \hat{\theta}) = \mathbb{E}_\theta L(\theta, \hat{\theta}) = \int L(\theta, \hat{\theta})\, dP_\theta.$$

where dP_θ is a probability measure parametrized by θ.

- For a scalar parameter θ and a quadratic loss function,

$$L(\theta, \hat{\theta}) = (\theta - \hat{\theta})^2$$

the _____ function becomes the mean squared error of the estimate,

$$R(\theta, \hat{\theta}) = E_\theta (\theta - \hat{\theta})^2$$

- In density estimation, the unknown parameter is probability density itself. The loss function is typically chosen to be a norm in an appropriate function space. For example, for L^2 norm,

$$L(f, \hat{f}) = \|f - \hat{f}\|_2^2$$

the _____ function becomes the mean integrated squared error

$$R(f, \hat{f}) = E\|f - \hat{f}\|^2$$

a. Financial modeling
c. Linear model
b. Risk
d. Risk aversion

7. A _____ in project management and systems engineering, is a tool used to define and group a project's discrete work elements (or tasks) in a way that helps organize and define the total work scope of the project.

A _____ element may be a product, data, a service, or any combination. A _____ also provides the necessary framework for detailed cost estimating and control along with providing guidance for schedule development and control.

a. Work breakdown structure
c. 1990 Clean Air Act
b. 33 Strategies of War
d. 28-hour day

8. _____ can be regarded as an outcome of mental processes (cognitive process) leading to the selection of a course of action among several alternatives. Every _____ process produces a final choice. The output can be an action or an opinion of choice.

a. 1990 Clean Air Act
c. 33 Strategies of War
b. 28-hour day
d. Decision making

9. _____ is the identification, assessment, and prioritization of risks followed by coordinated and economical application of resources to minimize, monitor, and control the probability and/or impact of unfortunate events.. Risks can come from uncertainty in financial markets, project failures, legal liabilities, credit risk, accidents, natural causes and disasters as well as deliberate attacks from an adversary. Several _____ standards have been developed including the Project Management Institute, the National Institute of Science and Technology, actuarial societies, and ISO standards.

a. Trademark
c. Succession planning
b. Kanban
d. Risk management

10. The _____ is a non-profit professional organization with the purpose of advancing the state-of-the-art of project management. The company is a professional association for the project management profession.

The _____ Inc.

a. 33 Strategies of War
c. 1990 Clean Air Act
b. 28-hour day
d. Project Management Institute

11. A _____ is a professional in the field of project management. _____s can have the responsibility of the planning, execution, and closing of any project, typically relating to construction industry, architecture, computer networking, telecommunications or software development.

Many other fields in the production, design and service industries also have _____s.

a. Project engineer
c. Work package
b. Project management
d. Project manager

12. The _____, is a mathematically based algorithm for scheduling a set of project activities. It is an important tool for effective project management.

It was developed in the 1950s by the Dupont Corporation at about the same time that General Dynamics and the US Navy were developing the Program Evaluation and Review Technique (PERT) Today, it is commonly used with all forms of projects, including construction, software development, research projects, product development, engineering, and plant maintenance, among others.

a. Critical path method
c. 33 Strategies of War
b. 1990 Clean Air Act
d. 28-hour day

Chapter 17. Project Management

13. The _____ Method is a tool for scheduling activities in a project plan. It is a method of constructing a project schedule network diagram that uses boxes, referred to as nodes, to represent activities and connects them with arrows that show the dependencies.

- Critical Tasks, noncritical tasks, and slack time
- Shows the relationship of the tasks to each other
- Allows for what-if, worst-case, best-case and most likely scenario

Key elements include determining predecessors and defining attributes such as

- early start date
- last-last
- early finish date
- late finish date
- Duration
- WBS reference

a. Project management office
c. Project manager
b. Precedence diagram
d. Work package

14. _____ is one of the four elements of marketing mix. An organization or set of organizations (go-betweens) involved in the process of making a product or service available for use or consumption by a consumer or business user.

The other three parts of the marketing mix are product, pricing, and promotion.

a. Job creation programs
c. Distribution
b. Matching theory
d. Missing completely at random

15. _____ is the self-government of a nation, country or some portion thereof, generally exercising sovereignty.

The term _____ is used in contrast to subjugation, which refers to a region as a 'territory' --subject to the political and military control of an external government. The word is sometimes used in a weaker sense to contrast with hegemony, the indirect control of one nation by another, more powerful nation.

a. A Stake in the Outcome
c. AAAI
b. A4e
d. Independence

16. _____ is a Japanese philosophy that focuses on continuous improvement throughout all aspects of life. When applied to the workplace, _____ activities continually improve all functions of a business, from manufacturing to management and from the CEO to the assembly line workers. By improving standardized activities and processes, _____ aims to eliminate waste .

a. Sensitivity analysis
c. Psychological pricing
b. Kaizen
d. Cross-docking

Chapter 17. Project Management

17. _____ is a business management strategy, initially implemented by Motorola, that today enjoys widespread application in many sectors of industry.

_____ seeks to improve the quality of process outputs by identifying and removing the causes of defects (errors) and variation in manufacturing and business processes. It uses a set of quality management methods, including statistical methods, and creates a special infrastructure of people within the organization ('Black Belts' etc.)

a. Six sigma
b. Theory of constraints
c. Takt time
d. Production line

18. _____ is a method of planning and managing projects that puts the main emphasis on the resources required to execute project tasks. It was developed by Eliyahu M. Goldratt. This is in contrast to the more traditional Critical Path and PERT methods, which emphasize task order and rigid scheduling. A Critical Chain project network will tend to keep the resources levelly loaded, but will require them to be flexible in their start times and to quickly switch between tasks and task chains to keep the whole project on schedule.

a. Precedence diagram
b. Critical Chain Project Management
c. Project engineer
d. Project management office

19. _____ is an advertisement in which a particular product specifically mentions a competitor by name for the express purpose of showing why the competitor is inferior to the product naming it.

This should not be confused with parody advertisements, where a fictional product is being advertised for the purpose of poking fun at the particular advertisement, nor should it be confused with the use of a coined brand name for the purpose of comparing the product without actually naming an actual competitor. ('Wikipedia tastes better and is less filling than the Encyclopedia Galactica.')

In the 1980s, during what has been referred to as the cola wars, soft-drink manufacturer Pepsi ran a series of advertisements where people, caught on hidden camera, in a blind taste test, chose Pepsi over rival Coca-Cola.

a. 28-hour day
b. Comparative advertising
c. 1990 Clean Air Act
d. 33 Strategies of War

20. A _____ -- also known as a geographically dispersed team -- is a group of individuals who work across time, space, and organizational boundaries with links strengthened by webs of communication technology. They have complementary skills and are committed to a common purpose, have interdependent performance goals, and share an approach to work for which they hold themselves mutually accountable. Geographically dispersed teams allow organizations to hire and retain the best people regardless of location.

a. Kanban
b. Trademark
c. Risk management
d. Virtual team

Chapter 18. Management of Waiting Lines

1. In economics, business, retail, and accounting, a _____ is the value of money that has been used up to produce something, and hence is not available for use anymore. In economics, a _____ is an alternative that is given up as a result of a decision. In business, the _____ may be one of acquisition, in which case the amount of money expended to acquire it is counted as _____.

    a. Cost
    b. Fixed costs
    c. Cost allocation
    d. Cost overrun

2. _____ is an advertisement in which a particular product specifically mentions a competitor by name for the express purpose of showing why the competitor is inferior to the product naming it.

This should not be confused with parody advertisements, where a fictional product is being advertised for the purpose of poking fun at the particular advertisement, nor should it be confused with the use of a coined brand name for the purpose of comparing the product without actually naming an actual competitor. ('Wikipedia tastes better and is less filling than the Encyclopedia Galactica.')

In the 1980s, during what has been referred to as the cola wars, soft-drink manufacturer Pepsi ran a series of advertisements where people, caught on hidden camera, in a blind taste test, chose Pepsi over rival Coca-Cola.

    a. Comparative advertising
    b. 33 Strategies of War
    c. 1990 Clean Air Act
    d. 28-hour day

3. _____ is one of the four elements of marketing mix. An organization or set of organizations (go-betweens) involved in the process of making a product or service available for use or consumption by a consumer or business user.

The other three parts of the marketing mix are product, pricing, and promotion.

    a. Matching theory
    b. Missing completely at random
    c. Job creation programs
    d. Distribution

4. In probability theory and statistics, the _____s are a class of continuous probability distributions. They describe the times between events in a Poisson process, i.e. a process in which events occur continuously and independently at a constant average rate.

The probability density function (pdf) of an _____ is

Here $>\lambda > 0$ is the parameter of the distribution, often called the rate parameter.

    a. AAAI
    b. A Stake in the Outcome
    c. A4e
    d. Exponential distribution

5. _____ of the learning curve effect and the closely related experience curve effect express the relationship between equations for experience and efficiency or between efficiency gains and investment in the effort. The experience of 'learning curves' was first observed by the 19th Century German psychologist Hermann Ebbinghaus according to the difficulty of memorizing varying numbers of verbal stimuli, and subsequent learning about the complex processes of learning are discussed in the

.

The rule used for representing the learning curve effect states that the more times a task has been performed, the less time will be required on each subsequent iteration.

a. Spatial Decision Support Systems
b. Point biserial correlation coefficient
c. Distribution
d. Models

6. In queueing theory, _____ is the proportion of the system's resources which is used by the traffic which arrives at it. It should be strictly less than one for the system to function well. It is usually represented by the symbol ρ.

a. AAAI
b. Utilization
c. A4e
d. A Stake in the Outcome

ANSWER KEY

Chapter 1

1. b	2. d	3. d	4. a	5. d	6. a	7. d	8. b	9. c	10. a
11. c	12. a	13. d	14. b	15. d	16. a	17. b	18. d	19. c	20. d
21. d	22. d	23. c	24. c	25. d	26. c	27. b	28. d	29. a	30. d
31. a	32. d	33. d	34. d	35. b	36. d	37. b	38. c	39. d	40. c
41. d	42. a	43. d	44. d	45. d	46. d	47. c	48. d	49. d	50. b
51. d	52. c	53. b	54. a	55. d	56. d	57. c	58. d	59. d	60. a
61. a	62. d	63. c	64. d	65. b	66. d	67. b	68. a	69. b	70. d
71. a	72. a								

Chapter 2

1. d	2. d	3. d	4. a	5. d	6. d	7. d	8. b	9. a	10. b
11. d	12. c	13. d	14. d	15. d	16. c	17. a	18. d	19. a	20. d
21. b	22. c	23. b	24. c	25. d	26. d	27. a			

Chapter 3

1. d	2. b	3. b	4. c	5. d	6. c	7. a	8. b	9. b	10. d
11. d	12. a	13. c	14. d	15. d	16. d	17. c	18. d	19. b	20. d
21. d	22. d	23. c	24. a	25. c	26. a	27. c	28. a	29. d	30. c
31. d	32. d	33. c	34. b	35. d					

Chapter 4

1. b	2. b	3. d	4. d	5. d	6. c	7. d	8. b	9. c	10. d
11. c	12. d	13. d	14. b	15. a	16. c	17. b	18. d	19. a	20. a
21. a	22. c	23. b	24. d	25. a	26. d	27. d	28. a	29. d	30. d

Chapter 5

1. d	2. a	3. d	4. d	5. c	6. b	7. b	8. b	9. d	10. c
11. b	12. d	13. d	14. a	15. d	16. b	17. d	18. d	19. c	20. c
21. b	22. b	23. a	24. d	25. d	26. b	27. d	28. d	29. d	30. d
31. b	32. a	33. d	34. d	35. d	36. d	37. d	38. c	39. b	40. b
41. d									

Chapter 6

1. a	2. d	3. d	4. a	5. a	6. b	7. d	8. d	9. d	10. b
11. b	12. a	13. d	14. a	15. b	16. a	17. c	18. d	19. d	20. d
21. c	22. d	23. c	24. d	25. b	26. d	27. d	28. d	29. d	30. a
31. a	32. c	33. d	34. d	35. d					

Chapter 7

| 1. d | 2. d | 3. b | 4. b | 5. a | 6. b | 7. a | 8. d | 9. b | 10. d |
| 11. d | 12. d | 13. a | 14. c | 15. b | 16. d | 17. b | 18. c | 19. d | 20. c |

Chapter 8

| 1. c | 2. d | 3. c | 4. c | 5. d | 6. b | 7. d | 8. d | 9. a | 10. a |
| 11. b | 12. d | 13. a | 14. d | 15. c | 16. d | 17. c | | | |

Chapter 9

1. b	2. a	3. c	4. a	5. d	6. a	7. c	8. a	9. d	10. a
11. c	12. d	13. b	14. d	15. d	16. d	17. c	18. c	19. d	20. b
21. d	22. d	23. a	24. b	25. c	26. d	27. d	28. c	29. d	30. c
31. b	32. d	33. d	34. d	35. d	36. b	37. d	38. d	39. a	

Chapter 10

1. d	2. b	3. a	4. b	5. a	6. b	7. a	8. d	9. a	10. c
11. a	12. d	13. c	14. a	15. d	16. b	17. b	18. d		

Chapter 11

1. d	2. d	3. d	4. a	5. d	6. d	7. d	8. d	9. b	10. d
11. b	12. b	13. d	14. b	15. b	16. d	17. b	18. b	19. c	20. b
21. d	22. d	23. a	24. d	25. c	26. b	27. d	28. d	29. b	30. d
31. b	32. a	33. d	34. a	35. d	36. a				

Chapter 12

1. c	2. d	3. b	4. d	5. b	6. d	7. a	8. d	9. d	10. d
11. a	12. c	13. c	14. d	15. d	16. b	17. d	18. d	19. d	20. a
21. a	22. a	23. a	24. b	25. a	26. b				

Chapter 13

1. d	2. c	3. d	4. d	5. b	6. d	7. d	8. c	9. d	10. d
11. d	12. a	13. a	14. b	15. c	16. d	17. d	18. c	19. d	20. d
21. d									

Chapter 14

1. d	2. c	3. a	4. c	5. c	6. d	7. b	8. b	9. b	10. d
11. d	12. a	13. c	14. b	15. d	16. d	17. c	18. d		

Chapter 15

1. d	2. d	3. c	4. d	5. d	6. d	7. b	8. d	9. d	10. a
11. b	12. d	13. b	14. d	15. c	16. d	17. c	18. d	19. d	20. d
21. d	22. d	23. d	24. d	25. c	26. d	27. a	28. a	29. a	30. a
31. c	32. c	33. a	34. b	35. d					

Chapter 16

1. c	2. d	3. d	4. b	5. c	6. d	7. b	8. b	9. b	10. a
11. d	12. b	13. a							

Chapter 17

1. d	2. a	3. c	4. b	5. d	6. b	7. a	8. d	9. d	10. d
11. d	12. a	13. b	14. c	15. d	16. b	17. a	18. b	19. b	20. d

ANSWER KEY

Chapter 18
1. a   2. a   3. d   4. d   5. d   6. b

www.ingramcontent.com/pod-product-compliance
Lightning Source LLC
Chambersburg PA
CBHW082048230426
43670CB00016B/2817